Women's World
Ideas and Procedures
for Missions Groups

Women's World Ideas and Procedures for Missions Groups

Dorothy Vander Kaay

REGULAR BAPTIST PRESS
1300 North Meacham Road
Schaumburg, Illinois 60173–4888

Library of Congress Cataloging-in-Publication Data
    Vander Kaay, Dorothy.
      Women's world ideas and procedures for missions groups.

      Rev. ed. of: Women's world handbook of ideas and
    procedures for ladies groups. 1974.
      1. Women in missionary work. I. Vander Kay, Dorothy.
    Women's world handbook of ideas and procedures for ladies
    groups. II. Title.
      BV2610.V36   1989   266'.0082   89-4001
      ISBN 0–87227–133–1

© 1989
Regular Baptist Press
Schaumburg, Illinois 60173-4888

Printed in the United States of America

To my dear husband, Louis, whose love and devotion for the Lord have made it possible for me to serve the Lord as a laywoman in the women's missionary activities of my church and Association. Without his patience and personal sacrifice through the years when our children were young, none of this would have been possible.

Contents

Foreword 9
Introduction. 11
1. The Need for Women's Missionary Groups 13
2. Missionary Group Goals. 16
3. Leadership 21
4. Starting a Missionary Group. 27
5. Purposeful Organization 30
6. Governing Rules 34
7. Conducting Business Meetings 39
8. The President 44
9. The Vice President 47
10. The Secretary 50
11. The Treasurer 56
12. Committees 59
13. Program Committee and Programming 66
14. Project Committee. 76
15. Project Order Form 81
16. Requisition Form 85
17. Personal Measurement Chart 89
18. Missionary Treasure Chest or Cupboard. 91
19. Project Suggestions for Women's Groups 98
20. Prayer Power in Women's Missionary Groups . . 104
21. The Missionary and the Missionary Group 110
22. The Individual Woman and the Women's
    Missionary Group 121
23. The Pastor's Wife and the Women's Group 126

24. The Women's Group and Missionary Education
    in the Church 132
25. The Women's Group and the Church Missionary
    Conference 135
26. Women's Meeting in the Wilderness (Skit) 140
27. A Checklist for Your Women's Group 151

Foreword

The author's ability to communicate with women at home and around the world is known and appreciated by countless numbers. For several years her column, "Women's World," appeared in the *Baptist Bulletin,* a monthly publication. Her practical suggestions and wise counsel rendered a great service to women's groups and missionaries everywhere.

The volume of mail received by Mrs. Vander Kaay has indicated the continuing need for this kind of help. With this encouragement, along with the verbal urgings of her host of friends, she has brought these articles together in one volume.

The subject matter of this book is of vital importance to every woman who desires to serve the Lord through the women's service group of her church. The governing rules for a purposeful organization, parliamentary procedures, responsibilities of officers and committees and project suggestions are clearly defined. This is a practical handbook that will become a "must" in every woman's library.

Introduction

Reading through the Old Testament of the Bible, we soon realize that women had an important part in Israel's history. A few examples are Sarah, the mother of a nation; Deborah, a judge of Israel; Hannah, the mother of Samuel; and the Shunammite woman, the one who provided for Elisha. Women are also prominent in the New Testament. There is Mary, chosen to bear God's Son; Dorcas, the seamstress; Euodias and Syntyche, helpers of Paul. There are many others, but these help us recall the place women have held in serving the Lord.

If it were possible to read a history of missions from its beginning up to the present time, we would see the role that women have also had in reaching the lost for Christ. Praise the Lord for the women who have gone to the fields of the world, but also for those who have done their part to enable others to go with the Good News. God calls some to go, but He also calls others to be faithful on the home front by praying, sewing, rolling bandages and using their many other abilities to further the work of missions. It would be difficult to accomplish these many things as individuals, but by meeting together in groups much can be done. Remember the old saying, "Many hands make light work."

Besides the projects done by ladies, there is another part that has equal importance—and that is prayer. There is not a missionary today who does not depend on the prayers of others. Ladies' groups can have a great ministry of prayer for the missionaries their churches support by sharing the prayer requests they receive from each field and then praying and continuing the work of intercession on a daily basis at home.

⅄ We cannot divide missions into "home" and "foreign." The field is the world, and America is a great and needy mission field as well. For one thing, people of many other nationalities are coming to our universities or are just migrating here. What an opportunity this brings to our own doorstep. The daily news reports also confirm to what extent Americans need to be reached with the gospel. If churches are not established here at home and church doors are not kept open, there will not be enough missionaries to go (or finances to send them) to the other fields of the world.

Having two children of our own on foreign fields today, my husband and I realize how important it is for them and their families to be upheld not only by finances from their supporting churches but also by heartfelt interest and prayer.

⅄ May we as Christian women let the Lord use us to further the cause of Christ by doing our parts to enable others to go to spread the Good News to every creature.

Donna Vermilyea
Continental Baptist Missions
Grand Rapids, Michigan

1 The Need for Women's Missionary Groups

Are women's missionary groups still needed to do work for missionaries? The answer is yes. Missionary groups are needed! They are needed if they will work and give sacrificially to provide the kind of equipment and supplies that are needed to carry on the work on mission fields.

There are large and beautiful modern cities on some of the faraway continents of the world; but, remember, surrounding every large city are villages, the countryside and even bush stations. Even in the United States, a country that is known for its many, many large cities, hundreds of villages have a population of fewer than two hundred. Some of these rural areas are hundreds of miles from a metropolis.

The large city is the exception for most missionaries. Often mountains, jungles, impassable rivers or poor roads are a barrier between the missionary and a shopping center. Prices are often high in the city marketplace, making it impossible for the missionary to stretch a limited budget to include even the necessities. Purchasing drugs, white cross supplies and bedding would be impossible in the quantity needed for a hospital or dispensary. The missionaries must depend upon the women at home.

The average American missionary is much larger than nationals in Asian countries like China and Japan. The clothing is made much smaller, and the missionary is not able to buy items right off the racks or shelves. The missionary needs the women at home to sew clothing.

Perhaps you are wondering whether anyone appreciates the work that your group is doing. For years you have been meeting each month to cut, sew, pack and mail projects to your missionaries. When the packages arrive at their destination, the missionaries write and thank you. You know that whatever you do, you are to do it "heartily, as to the Lord, and not unto men; knowing that of the Lord [you] shall receive the reward. . . ." But isn't it wonderful when we receive a bonus thank-you!

Several years ago I was introduced to Francois Siangar, a national pastor from the Republic of Chad. Because he could not speak English, I had to speak to him through an interpreter. What a thrill to hear his glowing testimony and to know that he was thankful for the work that has been done by the women in our churches. I asked him if he was aware that many women gathered in our churches each month to provide supplies for various mission fields. He said, "Oh, yes, we do appreciate all that the ladies do for our mission." He told us that he was saved because of the faithfulness of missionaries in the Chad and that many others will be saved. In speaking of one particular project, he said that the sacrifice made by the American women in our Regular Baptist churches has spread like a sweet perfume from a broken alabaster box over the Republic of Chad. He relayed many messages of thanks from fellow Christians in the Chad.

Mr. Siangar then opened the Word of God and expounded it with ease. He freely quoted Scripture passages. Mr. Siangar presented the need for more missionaries in the Chad and pled for young people to dedicate their lives for missionary service. Although he bore the scars of tribal rites inflicted on him as a child, his face radiated the love of Christ. As he stood on the platform, I thought, "Just suppose that mission stations in the Chad had been closed because of a lack of supplies or missionaries. What about Francois Siangar? Would he be a follower of some heathen deity instead of Christ?" (Pastor

Chapter 1

Siangar has since been martyred for his faith in Christ.)

If I could somehow portray the depth of his message to you, the women in our churches, I know that you would never wonder again if all the work is worth the effort. You would never again try to do missionary work with "junk." You would give sacrificially of yourself and money in order to send the very best equipment and supplies to be used in winning the lost.

Some groups have been persuaded that missionaries no longer need things that can be sewed or made by women in the churches. This is not true. Many missionaries have indicated that the women's missionary group is an important part of their work, not only for prayer support but as a source of needed supplies. The following letter from Mrs. William Carmichael, a missionary to the Republic of Mali with Evangelical Baptist Missions, expresses the feelings of our missionaries.

I have heard that our women's missionary groups are slowly disintegrating because many of the ladies feel that they and their work are not needed by missionaries. This distresses me because I feel that women's missionary groups are a real part of the missionary program.

Where would missions be today without women, both on the field and at home? Missionary interest is kept alive through the women's missionary groups in our churches.

The work which the ladies do is vitally needed on the mission field. Where would our dispensaries be without rolled bandages and squares, pill envelopes, and so forth, which you ladies have patiently rolled, folded and glued? What about rag rugs and quilts? Many items of clothing can be sewed. Handcrafts, items to be given out as prizes and visual aids are a real help and save your missionary the time involved in making them herself.

I believe that prayer interest is a vital part of your missionary meeting. The Lord has answered many prayers because ladies have prayed.

Writing letters to your missionaries is another important task. Many a day has been brightened and a missionary encouraged because of a cheerful letter from a prayer partner back home.

No, ladies, do not feel that your work is unimportant. We missionaries need you!

2 *Missionary Group Goals*

Many women's groups are missionary in name only. All too often fellowship has been substituted for a real and vital missionary vision. In some churches the monthly meeting has become a Bible study time. I am not disparaging Bible study or minimizing its importance, but it should not be used as a substitute for a missionary meeting.

Like the steeple, many women's missionary groups have become a traditional part of the church. In the past, forty or fifty years ago, or perhaps as recently as a decade ago, someone had a vision of what a group of women within a church could do for missions if they were organized to work and pray. As time has gone by, the vision has faded. Now all that is left is the organization, and meetings are planned to fill the time allotted to the group for its monthly meetings.

What can be done to give our groups purpose? If we could stand in the gap between life and eternity and look through the all-seeing eyes of God and see souls from every tribe and nation slipping in fear and anguish into a Christless eternity, perhaps it would give our groups purpose. We say we believe Hell is a place of eternal torment where the souls of men will live on, burning forever and ever. We say we believe Christ died on the cross to pay the price for the sins of the world. We know that God has given us the responsibility of reaching the uttermost parts of the world with the gospel. We say we believe all this—

and yet we confess that our missionary groups lack purpose! Pray that God will give your officers and your group a vision of the fields that are white unto harvest.

I suppose very few women in our missionary groups will ever go to a mission field. Yet we have been commissioned to go. What are we going to do with our commission? Have we stopped to think that prayer, our prayer, the prayer of our groups, can move men and kings and nations all over the world? A few of our missionaries have been coming home broken in body, some with nerves shattered. Some have given so much of their physical selves that they will never go back to the field; many are discouraged because souls are not being saved and national Christians are falling under Satan's attack. Others have been accepted by our mission boards but cannot go because of a lack of funds. Could it be that we have not been praying and claiming God's promise, "Call unto me, and I will answer thee, and shew thee great and mighty things, which thou knowest not"? The world has yet to feel the impact of a group of women dedicated to a ministry of intercession and provision of material needs. Many groups have fallen away from their original missionary vision because they neglected to seek God's guidance and direction for their activity. They prayed for guidance for the missionary on the jungle trail, but they did not pray for God's direction as to their next project, their officers or their month-to-month programming. Slowly but surely they have turned from their original purpose. These groups are a little like a football team playing on a field where all the yard lines have been obliterated and the goal posts have been destroyed.

Missionary groups need goals. If you have watched the great Olympic games, you have seen young people from many backgrounds gather to participate. The fact that there are many differences among them is obvious, even to the casual onlooker. They come from big cities and small hamlets. They are descendants of many races and nationalities. They have varying intellects and educational

17

experience. They come from different economic and social backgrounds. They often are unable to converse with one another because of language barriers. But there is one thing that they all have in common, and that is their goal. Every last one of them has the same goal, and they are there to win it—a gold medal.

Participants spend weeks, months and even years preparing for the competition. Every weight that could be a hindrance is laid aside. If long hair is a hindrance to winning the gold medal for swimming, the hair is cut. Clothing is not dictated by fad or style or even personal taste; it is chosen for its practicality and the fact that it could make a difference in whether the wearer wins the gold medal or the silver medal. Brawn and muscle are mute testimony to the fact that physical endurance has been developed the hard way by grueling exercise— engaged in faithfully in spite of tired, aching muscles—and much self-sacrifice.

Every participant has spent much time and energy seeking the best possible instruction from coaches and professionals. Hours and hours have been devoted to reading the stories of other gold medal winners. Equipment and gear have been examined thoroughly before decisions to use them have been made. Former record breakers have been watched on film to see how they succeeded. Rules have been reviewed and memorized to prevent the possibility of disqualification by default. The athletes have done these things because they have a goal in mind.

Some have entered the Olympics in years past and return to defend a title record and to earn another gold medal. Others have been there before and failed, but return to try again. Mistakes have been corrected, preparation increased, seconds lopped off previous records and another look has been taken at the gold medal waiting for the one person who has been willing to expend the effort to win it.

Monetary rewards are not directly involved. Entrants

will not receive money for their efforts. To the contrary, many have to raise their own funds in order to reach the Olympics. Why do they do it? They have a goal.

I imagine that thousands of young people have toyed with the idea of entering the Olympics, but they have not been willing to make the sacrifice and to pay the price. In this contest there is no room for halfhearted aspirants.

Our missionary groups need a goal. What is that goal? It is the laying of crowns at the feet of our Lord and Savior. It is the presenting of souls won to the Savior on mission fields around the world because of our prayer and material support of the missionaries sent out by our churches.

What has your group accomplished during the past year? What have you accomplished as a member of your group? How much have you done to help the missionaries carry out their work? How much have you really prayed? How many answers to prayer can be credited to your account? Are you willing to present the results of your efforts to the Lord as your part in seeking to reach the world with the good news of the gospel, or are you ashamed? Do you have to admit that you really have not tried very hard?

We listen to pep talks and we are enthusiastic for a while. We read materials about missions and ways to improve our groups, but we fail to act. We attend workshops to see what other groups are accomplishing, and we are excited at the possibilities; but we shake our heads and decide that it takes too much effort. We hear missionaries tell about their work and needs, and we shed a tear, but then we forget so soon. Halfhearted missionary groups are not good enough. They cannot get the job done.

What stands in the way of accomplishment for our groups? Many things prevent us from reaching the goal we have been talking about: lack of time, lack of interest, lack of money, lack of purpose, lack of vision, lack of willingness to expend the effort to do the job well and a lack of concern for reaching the lost with the gospel.

In the world of athletes there are scores of runners,

jumpers, discus throwers, swimmers, skiers and sprinters who are good—up to a point, but they are unwilling to make the sacrifices that would take them all the way to the gold medal. They are willing to watch someone else win the contest. Many women's groups are like that—good to a point, but unwilling to make the sacrifice that would change their organization and make it a real blessing to the missionary program of their church and faithful to God's Great Commission. Women complain because their groups are in a rut, but they are so prone to wait for someone else to do something about it.

Our missionary groups need women who are willing to step out from the crowd to serve the Lord in their own churches. We need women who are willing to sacrifice time and effort to prepare for the task of leading the women of our churches on to accomplish all that God intends for them to do in order to reach the world with the gospel. The ideas in this book have been compiled for those who want to help their missionary groups to have a more fruitful ministry for their missionaries.

You do not have to belong to a mediocre missionary group. You can change your group with the Lord's help if you are willing to be *the woman* that God can use to do His work. The material in this book will assist you in pulling your group out of the proverbial rut.

3 *Leadership*

Leadership is the most important factor in the success of any group or organization. I make this statement with full awareness of the prime importance of prayer and the spiritual tone of the meeting. All too often, however, we equate leadership with the task of moderating a meeting and no more. We think of leadership as being the ability to rap a gavel, follow an agenda and pronounce a meeting adjourned. This is only one phase of leadership.

Good leadership is aware of the group's purpose in being. Good leadership studies the constitution, former records and traditions of the group so that future goals can be determined and placed before the membership. Once the purpose of the group is known, the leadership should concentrate on a program of unification so that all of the organization's efforts are directed to fulfilling that purpose. Without unified purpose, the group will seem to be an octopus with tentacles leading in all directions.

Good leadership is the cooperative effort of all the elected officers and the appointed chairwomen. They combine their skills and abilities for the benefit of the organization, setting aside any desires they may have for personal accomplishment. It is the same sacrifice that the accomplished instrumental soloist makes when he assumes the position of leadership of an orchestra or band. He sets aside his own talent as a soloist and concentrates on developing and unifying a group of musicians. The greater their performance, the greater his satisfaction.

A good leader is not measured by her ability to do a lot of work. I am sure you are acquainted with at least one project chairwoman who takes all of the work home and does it herself. She may be capable of doing the work of several women, it is true, but she limits the potential capacity of the group by failing to share the work. If two heads are better than one, then certainly a dozen pairs of hands are better than one pair. Unless you learn to delegate, you will never be an effective leader. Moses received this good advice from his father-in-law. He accepted the wise counsel and was able to multiply his ability through the use of others. You must be able to delegate work, responsibility and authority. Now that I have used the word *delegate,* I hasten to explain that I am not speaking of autocratic rule. The leader who tells others what and how to do it without participating herself will receive very little cooperation. The leader must work cooperatively and in harmony with others. She must seek the assistance and advice of the membership in planning and carrying out the activities of the group. Leaders have to work shoulder to shoulder with the women as they direct the activities of the group. They have to do their share. They have to multiply themselves, their time and their ability by working through others.

Good leaders are aware of their responsibility. They make sure that nothing prevents the completion of their responsibility. I know many presidents and officers who do little more than conduct a business session. They are lax in planning, lax in publicity, lax in providing missionary education, lax in developing prayer effectiveness, lax in developing future leadership abilities of younger women and lax in the area of uniting the women of the church in the work and ministry of the missionary program.

Do you have any idea of the high cost of ineffective leadership in your women's group? It is the high cost of a soul, yes, of a hundred thousand souls a day who are sacrificed to an eternity without Christ because we are not equipping missionaries to do the work God has called them to do on home and foreign fields. Ineffective leadership causes the women of our churches to conclude that going to the missionary meeting is not important. Ineffective leadership will mean small attendance, small offerings, lack of interest and humdrum meetings.

If you are an officer or a committee chairwoman in your missionary group, you are a leader. What is a leader? Judging from the role of many officers, we must conclude that a leader can be *just* a mistress of ceremonies, a reader of reports or someone who fills an office.

Webster defines a leader as a person who leads; a director; a guiding head; a horse harnessed before all others in the same hitch. All of these definitions are applicable to officers and chairwomen.

If groups are going to GO and GROW, they must have good leaders. They must have direction. Someone to fill the position of a guiding head is an absolute must. The suggestion of being harnessed before all others in the same hitch aptly describes the leader of a group. She is not up in the driver's seat pulling the reins; she is in the harness along with the others, leading them on to accomplishment. Many groups have a lot of "horsepower," but it is unharnessed and little is accomplished. You have seen pictures of four, six or even eight horses hitched to a wagon. They are all headed in the same direction and there is a lead horse. Can you imagine a wagon with six horses but with some headed north, some south and some east or west? What a waste of horsepower. If they are going to make progress, they must all follow the lead horse and pull in the same direction. Many of our groups are like that—everyone is going her own way. There is no organized plan to follow. These groups have officers but no real leaders to guide. One year they go this way, and the next they go that way. The result is a waste of woman power.

If you are one of the leaders in the women's activities of your church, consider it a God-given privilege. Down through the ages God chose leaders to do His work. They were not always paragons of ability and perfection. Moses

23

is a good example. God did not call him because he had proved himself a great leader and because he had accomplished great feats in the leadership of men. Moses was only a shepherd hiding on the backside of the desert. He considered himself unworthy of the work God was calling him to do; and he said, "Who am I . . . that I should bring forth the children of Israel?" He told God about his lack of eloquence and inability to speak well. Moses did not become an important leader in Israel because of who he was as a person but because he was chosen of God and was willing to become an instrument to be used of God.

Every woman who serves in a position of leadership in her group should be very much aware that she is not a leader because she is important as a person; she should know that she is just a person being used of God as a leader to do His work. There is nothing that will do more to harm the growth of a group than a spirit of pride about one's position. Leaders must not lose sight of the fact that serving God is a privilege whether it is in the land of Egypt, leading two million Israelites to the Promised Land or in the smallest church in America, leading six or seven ladies to accomplish all that they can do to carry out the Great Commission.

As a leader, Moses faced discouraging times. He was often criticized and accused; he had to go through difficult places; he became tired and weary; he questioned why; he often had to stand alone. He became impatient with the unbelief and perhaps with the lack of vision of those he was leading. Moses did not throw up his hands and resign. No, his strength was in the Lord. He was out in front of that group with his eyes on the cloud by day and the pillar of fire by night. He was following God, and the Israelites were following him. If he had taken his eyes off the guiding cloud and turned around and listened to the crowd, he would have followed them back to Egypt! He would have been following instead of leading. The success of Moses' leadership was his ability to follow God. Your success as a leader of women in your church can also be measured by your ability to fix your eyes upon God and to follow Him, step by step, even when you become tired and discouraged. You should serve well because you are called of God.

You should also be mindful that the women of your church have entrusted their organization to you. They elected you to lead them forward as a group. Their success depends in a large part on you and the kind of leadership you give them. You can do the bare minimum and allow the group to come to a near standstill, or you can set your hand to the plow and determine with the help of God to do all that is humanly possible to further the work of the organization. There will be difficult times and problems, but if you keep your eyes on the Lord and always remember that you are serving Him, you will know the satisfaction of much accomplishment and a job done well. You alone can decide the type of leadership that you are going to give your group. You should determine to serve well because you were elected by your group.

You also have an obligation to the missionaries supported by your church. You are the link between the women of the church and the missionaries. They are dependent on you as a leader for the prayer support and the provision of material things that can be provided by the ladies of your group. If you fail as a leader, the link between the ladies and the missionaries will be broken; as a result, there will be a lack of prayer power and a lack of supplies for the work of the Lord on mission fields supported by your church. Your failure may be the cause of countless numbers of souls going into a Christless eternity. You need to serve well because your missionaries are dependent upon you.

Prayerfully measure your objectives with God's yardstick for service.

1. **Philippians 4:13:** "I can do all things through Christ which strengtheneth me."

2. **Colossians 3:23:** "And whatsoever ye do, do it

heartily, as to the Lord, and not unto men."

3. **Exodus 12:26:** Continually ask yourself, "What mean ye by this service?" Are you trying to get acclaim by doing an outstanding job as an officer, or are you doing an outstanding job as an officer in order to equip missionaries to carry the gospel to the lost?

4. **1 Chronicles 29:5:** When you have considered the above verse and admonition, you can freely ask, "Who then is willing to consecrate his service this day unto the LORD?"

5. **Romans 12:1:** Be willing to give of your service. "Present your bodies a living sacrifice." Give of the work of your hands and the things that you can do physically to work for missions.

6. **Ephesians 6:7:** Do not adopt a holier-than-thou attitude because you feel that you are doing more than others. Instead, "With good will doing service, as to the Lord" so that what you do will be a testimony and a blessing. *Remember that what you do is important; how you do it is a testimony.*

7. **Matthew 28:19 and 20:** Above all else keep the Great Commission ever before you, and always remember that it is the reason you have a missionary group to lead.

4 Starting a Missionary Group

A good start is as important to an organization as a foundation is to a building. Do not start out in a haphazard manner. Go slowly. Pray, ponder and plan before you proceed. In the beginning, you may have only five or six women in your church. Remember, however, your organization should be capable of meeting not only present needs but also projected growth. If the women of a small church are concerned about the lost on the foreign fields of the world, they will be concerned about the lost in their neighborhoods. Thus, growth is assured and must be considered in any plans you make for a women's missionary society.

All organizations within a church should exist only by permission of the church and should operate under the jurisdiction of the pastor and church board. Secure permission, therefore, to organize a new group before any plans are made. After you have received the authority to proceed, you may plan the first meeting. The place and purpose of the meeting should be announced publicly so that every woman in the church knows that she has the opportunity to participate. It is a mistake for a few women to do the planning and expect all to cooperate.

Seek the will of the Lord for your organization and His direction for every phase of the work and program. Begin your first meeting with a time of prayer.

You may want to have a speaker from a well-organized women's group, since much can be learned from the experience and mistakes of others. If a qualified speaker is not available to challenge your group, do some reading and prepare a report on what is being done and what can be done by a missionary group. Correspond with churches in other areas to find out what they are doing. Read books available on women's missionary groups.

At the initial meeting, consider these two basic questions:

1. *Why organize a missionary group in your church?* In other words, your proposed group should have a reason for existence. When I was a little girl, my friends and I organized a club every summer. We always started out by electing officers, finding a name and deciding the time and place to have meetings. After we completed these organizational details, we spent hours trying to figure out the purpose of the club. As is true of too many church women's groups, we had the organization but lacked a purpose. Many missionary groups are, in reality, Bible study groups, social societies or "ladies' aides." They do nothing for missions or missionaries. The purpose of a missionary group should be to pray for missions, to provide material needs of missionaries through offerings and work projects and to promote an interest and knowledge of missions within the group and church. What is your purpose?

2. *Should you organize a missionary group in your church?* Let the women express their honest feelings. Do they see the need for a missionary group? Will they support it with prayer, time and money? Will a majority of the women vote to organize? Discuss the project and program possibilities as well as the ideas and suggestions of the women present.

Set a date for the second meeting. Appoint a temporary chairwoman to preside and a nominating committee to prepare a slate of officers for election at the meeting. Perhaps you should also invite a missionary speaker to bring a challenge to your new group. It is important for you to know the missionaries' viewpoints on the need for women's missionary groups to carry out the Great Commission. The officers should meet soon after they are elected to prepare a proposed constitution and bylaws. For the most part, these documents set forth the group's organization and functions. Great care should be taken, therefore, in preparation. Make copies of the proposed constitution for all the women in the church. Ask them to read it prayerfully and to be present at the next meeting of the group to discuss it. Have the secretary record any suggestions or proposed changes so that the officers can evaluate the suggestions before the next meeting. At that meeting, the group should go over the documents point by point either to accept, to reject or to make changes in them. When completed, the constitution and bylaws should be adopted officially by the group.

Keep your organization simple. It is better to have two or three functioning committees than a dozen that do nothing. If you grow gradually, you will be able to keep abreast of everything. If you start out with a flash and try to do everything at once, you may find that you will lose control of everything.

5 *Purposeful Organization*

The success and effectiveness of missions around the world are dependent upon the vision of the local church. Our churches provide missionary personnel, prayer backing, financial support and material needs so that the gospel can be taken to the uttermost parts of the world. Properly organized women's missionary groups are an arm of the local church and share responsibility for its missions program. Many women's groups, however, are not carrying out their intended role. They are like the atrophied arm of the paralytic—present but not performing intended functions. We all need to check our groups periodically to make sure they are not slipping into the rut of purposeless organization.

Your constitution should state the PURPOSE of your group. If it does not, discuss the group's purpose and vote upon it. The purpose could read something like this: "Our purpose shall be to unite the women of our church and congregation in order that we may further the missionary program of our church by prayer and provision of material needs for our missionaries through offerings and work projects." Add the statement of purpose to the constitution by amendment if your present constitution so indicates, and safeguard the addition with the following provision: "The section of this constitution headed 'Purpose' cannot be amended."

The group should control not only its purpose but also its organization. Installing new officers every year or two is customary in most groups. And organizations rise or fall with the caliber of those elected. Some officers are "balls of fire," but others are halfhearted. Some are quite knowledgeable in areas of organization, programming and procedure; others lack know-how and have no desire to learn. The group is at the mercy of its elected officials unless provision is made for organizational uniformity. How can this uniformity be accomplished?

1. Prepare a list of officers and their duties.
2. Prepare a list of regular committees and their duties.
3. Prepare a list of simple parliamentary procedures that the group expects its officers to follow.
4. Prepare a meeting outline. This should not be the program but a "time-division" for regular meetings. In other words, a decision should be made by the group about the amount of time to allow for business sessions, barring unforeseen circumstances. Decide also how much time should be allotted for prayer instead of leaving this decision to individual prayer chairwomen. Many err by not having enough time for prayer. Others spend too much time talking about missionaries or reading long, detailed letters from them. Make a decision, too, about how much time should be set aside for work meetings. You should even decide how much time to spend on refreshments and fellowship. These guidelines, when adopted by the group, will prevent a problem that is common in many groups—lengthy preliminaries and business sessions with unproductive work meetings.

You may think of other areas that should be considered, but the important thing is that your group consider its organization, decide how it wants that organization to be run and then insure control of organization by vote. Then include the group's decisions in a document entitled

31

"Rules of Procedure." These rules can be adjusted from time to time as the need arises by a majority vote of the group. A new pastor always brings with him new ideas that he incorporates within the broad framework of the organization that already exists. New officers in a women's group should do the same. They will have new ideas, but they can work them out within the established organization of the group instead of changing the organization. The women's group belongs to the women of the church, and the officers and committee chairwomen serve the organization.

Many officers and committee chairwomen fail because they do not know what is expected of them. Remember, most of us are called upon only once or twice during our lifetimes to hold an office or committee chairwomanship. Our groups, therefore, are almost continually under the leadership of trainees. We learn while we serve. Then just when we finally know how to lead our groups, our terms expire. Valuable time is wasted after each installation of new officers or appointment of new committees. There is almost always that period of floundering in an effort to find out what is expected. Instead of electing a new group of officers and then waiting for them to tell you what they expect of the group in carrying out their ideas, try a system of controlling organization. Present new officers and chairwomen with a notebook of each office or committee. Include a constitution, rules of procedure and a detailed list of duties for each job. Also include rules of simple parliamentary procedure and indicate the group's desire in the area of "time-division." This notebook will not prevent creative, progressive thinking and ideas; rather, it will provide a solid base for new officers to build upon during their term.

Why do so many women refuse positions of leadership? I believe it is because they are afraid. They are unacquainted with proper procedure and would rather say no than make a mistake. Good officers will train those who work with them so that they can serve in an official capacity in the future. Plan a session prior to the appointment of the nominating committee each year to review the constitution, the qualities of a good leader and information about conducting a business meeting. List the duties of each officer and show the women in the group the material each officer receives to guide and help her in her office. In addition, have available for your group a copy of *Robert's Rules of Order.*

6 *Governing Rules*

The importance of the constitution or bylaws of an organization cannot be overemphasized. If the business of a group is to be conducted in an orderly fashion, there must be a set of rules to guide the officers and membership. The constitution protects the rights of the members of a group. We often make the mistake of thinking that only large, formal groups need a constitution. This is not true. The smallest organized group needs governing rules.

When the membership of an organization adopts a constitution, it makes provision to grant certain powers to its elected officials. By the same token, it also limits those powers. In addition, it insures equality of privilege to every member. It thus protects the group from change of purpose.

A constitution is binding once it has been adopted. Great care should be exercised in forming it. Nothing should be placed in the constitution that is of a temporary nature or subject to periodic change. For example: Do not state in the constitution that the group will meet on the fourth Thursday of every month. If Christmas falls on the fourth Thursday, the constitution would have to be amended in order to change the time of meeting. Rules of this type should be listed in the rules of procedure. These rules can be changed at any meeting without previous notice if there is a majority vote.

No provision of the constitution may be suspended for any reason. When the constitution states that voting must be by ballot, it is providing the membership with the privilege of privacy. This rule cannot be suspended unless the constitution states that it may be suspended by a unanimous vote of the members present.

If you are going to limit the term of office of elected officers, you should also provide for an emergency that may be created if there is no replacement for that office at the time of the election. The rule should provide that "Officers may hold an office for _____ terms or until their successors are elected."

The constitution should be preserved. Some groups have never adopted a set of governing rules. Others have had a constitution in years past but it has been lost in the process of changing officers, and so forth. Every new officer should receive a copy of the constitution at the time of election. This copy should be passed on to new officers along with other papers and records pertinent to the office. Sufficient copies of the rules of procedure should be on hand so that all members of the group may have a copy.

SAMPLE CONSTITUTION
Adopted   (date)

ARTICLE 1—NAME
The name of the organization shall be_____.

ARTICLE 2—PURPOSE
Our purpose shall be to unite the women of our church and congregation in order that we may further the missionary program of our church by
A. Prayer.
B. Provision of material needs for our missionaries through offerings and work projects.
C. Presentation of a program of missionary information and education for the ladies of the church.

ARTICLE 3—POLICIES
A. The group shall abide by all rules and policies that govern our church and its organizations.

B. No fund raising projects shall be conducted by or for our group.

C. The group shall not assume provision of salary support for any missionary or organization.

D. All projects for missionaries or organizations outside of those supported by our church must be approved by the church board.

ARTICLE 4—MEMBERSHIP

All women of the church, congregation and Sunday School are entitled to membership.

ARTICLE 5—VOTING

All group members in good and regular standing may vote. To be in good and regular standing, a member must attend a minimum of six meetings during a year.

ARTICLE 6—ORGANIZATION

A. Officers: president, vice-president, secretary, treasurer.

B. Qualifications:
   1. Any woman who has been a member of our church for at least one year and who is in good and regular standing in the church and missionary group is eligible to hold an office.
   2. No person shall hold concurrent offices in this group and another missionary group in this church.

C. Nominating Committee:

   A nominating committee shall be elected by the membership of the group at least one month prior to the election for the purpose of preparing a slate of officers. The slate shall be presented for election at the annual meeting. Further nominations may be made from the floor.

D. Elections:

   An election shall be held annually in (*month*). A majority of all votes cast shall be necessary to elect. The vote shall be by written ballot. The written ballot may be set aside by unanimous vote when there is but one candidate for an office.

Chapter 6

E. Term of Office:

Term of office shall be for one year and shall run from (*month*) to (*month*). Officers may serve for more than one term. (A recommended period is from September to September.)

F. Vacancies:

When a vacancy occurs, the remaining officers shall have the power to appoint a replacement to fill the unexpired term.

G. Duties:

1. *President*—The president shall call and preside over meetings of officers and regularly scheduled sessions of the group. She shall be a member ex officio of all committees except the nominating committee. She shall prayerfully lead the group with the aid of the other officers.

2. *Vice President*—The vice president shall assume the duties of the president in her absence.

3. *Secretary*—The secretary shall keep minutes of all regular meetings. She shall keep a record of minutes of officers' meetings. She shall handle correspondence as requested by the officers.

4. *Treasurer*—Offerings shall be received and held in trust by the treasurer. Monies shall be counted by the treasurer in the presence of one other member of the group. All monies shall be deposited with the church treasurer. [Some groups have their own bank accounts in which case the money would be deposited in their accounts.] Monies shall be disbursed upon recommendation of the officers and by approval of the membership. A legible set of double entry books shall be kept, showing itemized receipts and disbursements.

H. Meetings of Officers:

The officers shall meet at regular intervals to plan the work and meetings of the group.

I. Committees:

Committees shall be appointed by the officers when

it is necessary to do so.

ARTICLE 7—PARLIAMENTARY PROCEDURE

Unless the constitution provides otherwise, the group shall be governed by *Robert's Rules of Order.*

ARTICLE 8—PRACTICE

This constitution may be read aloud annually at the time of the election.

ARTICLE 9—AMENDMENTS

This constitution may be amended by a two-thirds vote of all those present at any regular business meeting, provided that notice of the proposed change and time of the meeting is made at least one month in advance of that meeting.

7 *Conducting Business Meetings*

Most of us have sighed through at least one long, drawn-out and pointless business session. We know that a lack of knowledge of proper procedure and a tendency to permit too much informality is the cause of confusion.

The success of an organization depends upon its president and the other officers. By the same token, an incompetent leader must accept the responsibility when the group falls short.

Perhaps you are wondering if only a gifted few are capable of holding these offices. The answer is no! Good presidents and officers are not born—they are developed. If you are willing to put forth the effort and take the time to prepare yourself, you can become a good officer.

The officers should study the constitution thoroughly to make themselves fully aware of its provisions. The constitution should be available at every business or executive meeting. Many of our women's groups are so loosely organized that a constitution has never been adopted. Other groups have lost their governing rules, and new officers carry on unaware that they exist. Every organization needs governing rules. Every group that is without a constitution should appoint a committee to prepare and present a suggested constitution and bylaws for approval and adoption. As soon as the constitution is adopted, it becomes the undisputed governing policy of the organization and can be changed only by amendment.

Preparation for the business meeting is extremely

important. If a meeting is worth the time given to it, it is worth the time it takes for preparation. Do not underestimate the worth of officers' meetings. When officers do not meet as a group to pray, to plan and to make decisions, they work as independent individuals each performing her required duty. When the president presides at a meeting, she represents all of the officers and their ideas. Remember, no one officer is more important than another. No president has the right to propose or dispose of matters without the consent of the officers as a group.

The president or someone appointed by her should make sure that all officers and committee heads have their reports and minutes ready for presentation at the meeting. When the chairwoman calls for a report and no one responds, the members soon become aware of a lack of preparation on the part of the officers. Lack of preparation indicates a lack of interest. A lack of interest is contagious.

The meeting should start on time. The chairwoman and anyone speaking should be easily heard. A good presiding officer is considerate of those who may have difficulty hearing. She is concerned for the comfort of those present. If the room is too warm or too cold, necessary adjustments should be made. She welcomes visitors and tries to make everyone feel at home. Before the meeting is called to order, the secretary assumes her place near the chairwoman. A good secretary records notes as the meeting progresses instead of relying on her memory later.

The presiding officer calls for order by rapping the gavel or announcing, "The meeting will please come to order." When she has secured the attention of all present, she proceeds with the agenda (a list of matters to be taken up at the meeting, arranged in logical order).

SAMPLE AGENDA
  1. Opening song and prayer
  2. Roll call of officers and membership
  3. Reading of minutes of previous meeting

4. Reading of letters and communications
5. Treasurer's report
6. Unfinished business
7. Reports of officers and committees
8. New business
9. Adjournment

Most, if not all, of our women's missionary groups have only a few simple parliamentary rules to govern their meetings. The biggest problem for the average president is correct terminology. The following will help you to conduct a meeting.

REPORTS
After the meeting has been called to order, the first item of business is the reading of reports. The president asks each officer in turn for her report. After the secretary reads the minutes, the president says, "You have heard the reading of the minutes; are there any additions or corrections?" Any member of the group may respond. If there is no response, the president announces, "There are no additions or corrections; the minutes stand approved as read." If there are any additions or corrections, they must be acted upon to the satisfaction of the membership. After all corrections and additions have been made, the president announces, "If there are not further corrections or additions, the minutes as corrected stand approved."

After the treasurer reads her report, the president asks, "Are there any questions regarding this report?" The treasurer is given opportunity to answer any questions that are raised. After all questions have been answered, the president says, "The treasurer's report is received and shall be filed." The annual written treasurer's report should be adopted by resolution after it has been audited by the church treasurer. This is done by a member of the group making the following resolution, "I move the acceptance of the treasurer's report." You may want to add the words "with thanksgiving to God." The president then calls for a second to the motion, and she takes a vote. There is no need for discussion or debate.

When committee reports are given and include a resolution, the proper course is for the person reading the report to move the adoption of the resolution. A second is made from the floor, and the discussion proceeds.

MOTIONS

The following is a brief outline showing how a motion should be handled:

1. *Obtaining the floor*—A member stands and addresses the chair by saying, "Madam president, may I speak?" The president then says, "The chair recognizes Mrs. Jones."

2. *Making the motion*—When Mrs. Jones has the floor, she says, "I move that _____." She then sits down to await further action.

3. *Seconding the motion*—Before Mrs. Jones' motion can be acted upon, another member must "second" her motion. This is done without leaving the seat or addressing the chair. If there is no second, the president announces that the motion is lost for want of a second.

4. *Statement of motion*—After the motion is seconded, the president asks the secretary to repeat the motion to the group. (The secretary should take great care in recording the motion exactly as it is given. She should include the name of the person making the motion and the name of the one who seconded it.)

5. *Discussion*—The members of the group are given opportunity to discuss or debate the motion. (The presiding officer has to keep the discussion centered on the motion. It is very easy to lose track of the subject in a discussion of this type.)

6. *Calling for the question*—If the president feels the discussion is lasting too long without accomplishment, she can call for the question; or any member

of the group can call for the question by rising, addressing the chair and asking for the question. (This means that the chair is being asked to put the motion to a vote.)

7. *The vote*—The president restates the motion so that it is clear to all who vote. Opportunity is given for the group to vote by a yes or no vote, a roll call vote or a vote by ballot. (When the constitution provides that a vote be by ballot, it must always be a written vote allowing members the privilege of privacy. If this rule is a part of the group's constitution, it cannot be suspended, even by a unanimous vote.)

8. *Announcement*—The president announces the result of the vote. The president should never put a motion to a vote unless she is sure that it is understood by everyone present.

9. *Amending a motion*—There are times when the original motion is changed by adding, leaving out or substituting something. The person amending the motion says, "I move to amend the original motion to provide that _____" (stating the change). When the amended motion is seconded, it is entitled to discussion and debate. The president announces that the amended motion must be voted on before the original motion. If there are two amendments, the last amendment is voted on first. If it loses, the first amendment is voted on. If the first amendment loses, the original motion is voted on. If one of the amendments is accepted by the group, the final vote is on the original motion as changed by the accepted amendment.

8 *The President*

More than any other elected officer, the president is responsible for the leadership of the missionary group. All other officers and committee chairwomen must wait for her instruction before moving ahead to perform their assigned duties. It is the president who calls the officers into session to make plans for the group. If she fails in this area, the officers do not meet and consequently do not carry out their functions. The president's responsibilities are listed in the sample constitution in the chapter on "Governing Rules" as follows: "The president shall call and preside over meetings of officers and regularly scheduled sessions of the group. She shall be a member ex officio of all committees except the nominating committee. She shall prayerfully lead the group with the aid of the other officers."

This concise description of responsibility leaves much unsaid. It omits the more detailed listing of duties that makes the difference between the president who gives the group good leadership and the president who just presides. Read the chapter on "Leadership." It describes the functions of leaders in general but can be applied to the office of the president in particular.

The president of a group should be spiritually mature and faithful in prayer and Bible reading in her own personal life. She should have a praying and working interest in the program of missions before she is elected to an office. This interest should be evidenced by her faithful attendance and participation in the work of the missionary group. Being elected to an office in the missionary group does not mean that the officer is automatically injected with an instantaneous missionary vision. If that vision is not present before the election, it is quite doubtful that it will be apparent during the term of office unless the officer is convicted of her lack in this area. This office does not belong to a novice. Many groups make the mistake of thinking that a disinterested woman can be drawn into the group and that she will attend the meetings if she is elected to hold an office. This is rarely true, and it can do a great deal of damage to the group during the term.

The president is the presiding officer of the group, and the woman who accepts the office has an obligation to prepare herself to preside properly. Some presidents make light of their lack of knowledge in this area and assume that they can lead their meetings in a haphazard fashion. This is not acceptable. As soon as an officer is elected, it is her responsibility to leave no stone unturned in an effort to find out how to preside and to conduct meetings. She should read all available material on parliamentary procedure and contact former presidents who have been successful. Furthermore, she should consult the pastor's wife. The pastor and missionary committee should be asked for information about the missionaries and missionary program of the church. It is inexcusable for an officer to acknowledge that she did not know what she was doing until she was at the end of her term. She does not have to spend a whole term learning by trial and error. The president should make sure that she knows how to preside before the first meeting of her term. It will take a little time and effort, but it can be done; and the women of your group will appreciate your sacrifice. This book is designed to help you handle your meetings in an interesting and productive manner.

The president should lead the group in an effective prayer ministry. Helpful suggestions are in the chapter entitled "Prayer Power." How encouraging it would be to your missionaries if they were notified that your group had dedicated themselves to a ministry of daily prayer support.

The president with the help of the other officers is responsible for the successful operation of all appointed committees. It is not enough to make the appointment. She must make sure that each committee functions and fulfills its assigned task.

9 *The Vice President*

The first and most important duty of a vice president is the difficult assignment of always being prepared to replace the president in the event of her absence from a single meeting or to replace her for the remainder of a term if circumstances force her retirement from the office. This means that the vice president should constantly be aware of the president's plans for the group and the business that is to be conducted. She may never need to use this knowledge, but she should always be prepared to step in if the need arises. The president, therefore, should keep the vice president informed at all times. Much of the responsibility for the vice president's success in carrying out her duties lies with the president. If the president does not keep the vice president well informed, she will not be able to act in an emergency.

We are all familiar with the following nominating committee jargon: "May we put your name up for vice president? There is nothing to do." In some instances the vice president automatically becomes the chairwoman of the refreshment committee, the publicity committee or the calling committee, so the nominating committee member says, "May we put your name up for vice president? All you have to do is make sure the refreshments are served. You are so good at planning meals that you were the first one we thought of for vice president." All too often the vice president is selected because of her culinary know-how and not for her executive ability.

The Vice President

It is not uncommon to hear a vice president say, "Me conduct the meeting tonight? Oh, no! I'm scared to death to speak in front of a group. You'll have to ask someone else." Or, "Me conduct a business meeting? I don't know the first thing about it. I don't know anything about motions or anything else and, besides, I have to be in the kitchen during the business session in order to get the refreshments ready."

Remember, the vice president you elect may be your president before the term is over. Select her because of her ability to preside at a meeting, her knowledge of parliamentary procedure, her ability to direct the group's activities and her ability to work with other women. The last point is very important, not only for the president and vice president, but for all officers.

If the vice president is to be the chairwoman of another committee, it should not keep her from being present during the business session of the group. She should not be in the kitchen brewing coffee after the gavel is rapped.

If an unusual circumstance arises and both the president and vice president are absent from the meeting, then the secretary would automatically take over as the presiding officer until the group appoints a chairwoman pro tem. After this procedure is completed, the secretary assumes her role as secretary for the meeting.

Soon after the election, the new president and vice president should meet to discuss their respective duties. They should become familiar with the group's constitution, basic parliamentary procedure (a copy of *Robert's Rules of Order* will answer many questions about motions, substitute motions, seconds, amendments, voting and so forth), and their relationship as leaders of the group. No president should work with a vice president for six months and then be surprised to hear, when the president has an appendectomy on the night of the group's meeting, that the vice president refuses to preside because she "doesn't know how." She should know this as soon as they begin to work together, and she should make sure the vice presi-

48

dent is prepared to assume the responsibility if necessary. If the vice president is uncertain or has questions, she should discuss the problem with the president and seek her guidance.

The vice president should be informed of the duties of the office before she is elected. If she is incapable or unwilling to serve not only as the vice president but also as the president if it becomes necessary, she should not accept the office.

10 The Secretary

The selection of a good secretary is extremely important to any organized group. More than one president has complained about the quality of the minutes kept by the secretary. The following example is an illustration of poorly written minutes. "The meeting opened with prayer by our president. The secretary's minutes and treasurer's reports were read and voted on. There was a discussion about the next project. The meeting closed with prayer." These minutes record nothing of what really took place at the meeting. They do not state where and when the meeting was held. We know the secretary's and treasurer's reports were read and voted upon, but we do not know the result of the vote. There was also a discussion about projects, but we do not know what action, if any, was taken. Minutes of this type serve no purpose.

Not everyone is able to serve in the capacity of a secretary. Some women find that writing is a very difficult task, and they should not accept the position of a secretary. For example, I never accept invitations to sing because I am unable to carry a tune. Perhaps I should say I would never accept such an invitation, since no one has ever asked me to sing. Others are aware of my lack of ability. On the same basis, not everyone has the ability to be a secretary. Choose this officer because of her ability and not her personality.

Secondly, the president should be careful to do her part in making the work of the secretary as easy as possible. Many times a group discusses a question for a long time, and the decision comes when there is no longer a protest to the subject. The president assumes that the silence is an affirmative vote. Every question under discussion should be in the form of a motion with a second and a vote by the group. The secretary should be instructed to record this procedure. If there is no vote, she can do little more than say, "There was a discussion."

If the president is asking for motions, seconds and votes, but the secretary is not recording them properly, she should ask the secretary after each motion, "Did you get that motion?"

The secretary should make her reports as complete as possible. She should seat herself at a table placed close to the presiding officer and take notes as the meeting progresses, always noting the name of the person making a motion and the one who seconds it. She should copy the motion, word for word, even if she has to ask that it be repeated. After the secretary has recorded the motion, she reads it aloud to the group to make sure everyone understands it before it is discussed and voted upon. The result of the vote is always recorded. The secretary should remember to record only what is done at the meeting and not what is said by the members in discussion.

It is very important for the secretary to make complete notes *during* the meeting. Many times the secretary's report is in error because she has tried to remember what was done several weeks after the meeting when she finally takes time to record the minutes. Another problem is the temptation to interpret what has been said and done. The secretary should not make personal comments, criticisms or observations in her minutes.

Well-written minutes should contain the following: (1) Kind of meeting: regular monthly or special annual, etc. (2) Name of the group. (3) Date of meeting and place where it was held. (4) Name of the presiding officer and her position. (5) Name of person opening the meeting with prayer. (6) Record of the reading of the previous meeting's minutes and treasurer's report and action taken by the group. (7) Record of committee reports presented to the group and any action taken on these reports. (8) Word by word statement of all motions and the name of the person making them. Names of those making seconds. Result of the vote on each motion. (9) Adjournment.

An example of a recorded motion is as follows: "Moved by Mary Smith and seconded by Betty Jones that the J.O.Y. group purchase a pair of pinking scissors at a cost of $7 for the project committee to use. Motion carried by a unanimous vote." It is not necessary to indicate that it was voted upon after much discussion or that it was suggested that we get them with trading stamps or any other comments made during the debate time.

When the secretary reads the minutes, she should stand, face the group and hold the notebook up so that she can project her voice to the last row in the room. The officer who talks into her collar will not be heard. Practicing before a mirror may help you to do a better job. If you have a tape recorder, try practicing with it. It will reveal whether you are enunciating clearly, speaking too softly or talking too fast. If you have to read a missionary letter aloud to the group, be sure to practice before the meeting. Sometimes it is difficult to read someone else's handwriting, especially if there are strange words and names. You may want to retype or underscore parts of the letter to make them easier for you to read to the group.

In most women's missionary groups the secretary handles the correspondence. It is important that this be done well as the secretary represents her group and her church. I have had correspondence from secretaries of missionary groups who have written on pieces of torn notebook paper, soiled or smudged stationery and even on pieces of brown paper torn from a shopping bag. On the other hand, I have received very neat notes on attractive but inexpensive stationery. The group should select stationery that they would like the secretary to use to represent them. If the secretary has a problem with her handwriting, it would be wise for her to secure the use of a typewriter.

Some presidents try to save time by eliminating the reading of reports. This is not wise. Reports are important and should be read or handed out in printed form at each meeting. A good rule of thumb is this: If you have a business session, read the reports. Special meetings, such as a mother and daughter program or a fellowship supper, would be an exception to this rule.

The secretary's report is valuable not only for the meeting at which it is read but for future meetings and decisions of the group. The minutes record a history of the women's group and its actions.

Minutes should be typed or written neatly and filed in a notebook. The current secretary's records should contain minutes for the past two or three years. The minutes should never be discarded. Preserve them carefully from year to year and file them in a safe place, perhaps with church historical records. Several years ago in one church, a new secretary decided that the notebook was too full and threw the old records into an incinerator. No officer or group of officers should assume responsibility for destroying the group's official records.

Since many women's groups conduct very little business, the presiding officer may skip records that seem unimportant and contain very few motions and actions of past meetings. This should not be done. All business is important to the group. In the past I have said that officers are elected to lead a meeting and not to make the decisions without action by the group. If a secretary and treasurer are elected, they should be given the opportunity to carry out their duties.

Some groups have combined the office of secretary and treasurer to eliminate the need for one officer and to increase the amount of work being done by the individual officer. I question that this is of any particular benefit to the organization. There are many things that can be done by the secretary to improve the group, although no secretary should be asked to do all the jobs suggested here. Committees can be appointed to help.

1. Keep an attendance record. Send cards to all absentees. (Watch the attendance grow.)

2. Plan interesting announcements of the group's activities for the church bulletin.

3. Address airmail stationery forms or regular envelopes to all of your missionaries. Distribute among members who are willing to write to a missionary.

4. Duplicate all missionary letters, staple together, and give to all the members of the congregation.

5. Prepare reports about each missionary supported by your church. Include information about the missionary and his family. Tell about their field of service—its people, customs, climate, political problems, education. Tell about the type of work being done by the missionary.

    Write to the missionary for this information or secure it from some member of his family here at home. You can also write to our mission boards to secure information about the work missionaries are doing on various fields around the world. Most of our mission boards have periodical publications and brochures about each of their mission fields.

    Read the report at a meeting to acquaint your group with the missionary and mission board. Or prepare true and false statements or questionnaires to be filled out by the group. Read the answers aloud. One group I attended had a spelldown of information about the missionaries and mission boards supported by that church.

6. Keep an itemized list of all work done by each

committee. Include the total number of quilts, bandages, dresses, etc., that are completed at each meeting. This will be of help in making out the annual report for the group.

7. Prepare a file or notebook of good ideas for the missionary group. Include sewing hints, project suggestions, devotional ideas, organizational information, statistical information about missions, etc.

8. Prepare a bulletin board of pictures of each missionary. (Use prayer cards.) Display it at each meeting to make sure everyone is acquainted with your missionaries.

11   *The Treasurer*

The duties of the treasurer may vary in different groups, but in the majority of cases she receives offerings and monies intended for the use of the group. She counts, records and deposits the money in the organization's bank account. It is wise for the treasurer to count the offerings and make the recording of the amount received in the presence of another member of the group. This is not done because of mistrust; but, in the event of error, the treasurer is protected by a witness. Some groups do not have a bank account, and the treasurer keeps the money in a drawer in her home. This is not a good policy. If someone should break into the home of the treasurer and take the money, there is always the question of responsibility. In addition, it puts temptation before the officer.

In one secular women's organization, the treasurer needed some change to pay the paper boy and she took it, planning to put it back. This happened on several occasions, and soon the sum was too large to replace. The group was out the money. The woman, shamed by her action, left the organization and dropped all friendships with anyone who had knowledge of the incident. If this had happened in the church, the results would have been far more tragic. It could mean that a whole family would no longer be in the church and Sunday School.

The treasurer should issue receipts for all funds received except in the offerings. She should not disburse money unless officially authorized. She should retain receipts given to her for payment of bills. She should keep a legible set of double entry books that are up-to-date at all times. The books should be open to any member who has a question about the finances of the organization. The books should be audited by the church treasurer or auditor each year. The treasurer should give reports at regularly scheduled meetings of the organization and when requested at board meetings. These reports are given for the information of the group and should be filed and not accepted like other committee reports, except for the report of the auditor.

The following report form is good for the treasurer to use in the average missionary group. The group should not permit its treasurer to scratch a few numbers on any old sheet of paper. These reports are very important to the group.

REPORT OF THE TREASURER OF THE WOMEN'S MISSIONARY SERVICE GROUP FOR MONTH ENDING JANUARY 31, 19__

GENERAL FUND

RECEIPTS
    Balance on hand December 31, 19__ . . . . $ 60.00
    January offering . . . . $ 20.00
    Special gift.   5.00
                                                                     25.00

TOTAL . . . . $ 85.00

DISBURSEMENTS
    Sewing committee for supplies . . . . $ 2.00
    Speaker for January meeting 10.00
    Shepherds for Dollar-A-Month Project . .   12.00
    Postage 2.50
                                                                     26.50

Balance on hand in General Fund January 31, 19__ $58.50

DIME BANK FUND

RECEIPTS
    Balance on hand December 31, 19__ .... $ 72.10
    Received....................... <u>$ 18.00</u>
                                     18.00

TOTAL .... $ 90.10

DISBURSEMENTS
    Sent to State Treasurer for Dime Bank
    Project 90.10
                                        $<u>90.10</u>

    Balance on hand January 31, 19__ 00.00

    Balance in all funds on January 31, 19__ ...... $ 58.50

12 Committees

The women's missionary group should be fully aware of the importance of committees in the work of an organization. Committees should not be appointed as a last resort when officers find that they cannot do the work themselves. Certain standing committees should be a part of an organization. A group will never meet its full potential if committees are not used wisely to facilitate the work.

The president of the United States is the executive head of our government, but he operates through scores of department heads. The president is unable to carry on government functions without the help of a cabinet and hundreds of aides and department heads. A good president selects top-notch cabinet members and assistants. When they do a good job, the president receives credit for wise leadership.

Every missionary group, large or small, should operate in the same manner. Good leadership will mean good working committees and much accomplishment. If the president does all the work herself, she will not have time to lead. If she leads and uses committees, she will not have to do all the work.

A missionary group can use both the standing committee and the special committee to carry out its work. Special committees are appointed to handle a specific need, such as the nominating committee. The special committee ceases to exist as soon as it has given its report to an organization and the report has been received.

The standing committee is most often used. This committee usually serves throughout a year. The following list may help to guide your thinking as to possible areas that can be handled by a standing committee: publicity; white cross; sewing; quilting; membership; program; cheer and aid; prayer and handwork.

The officers of your group should meet to discuss its needs and to set up a system of committees. The kind and number of committees will depend on the size of your group and the type of meetings you conduct.

Before you appoint committee members, prepare a list of duties and responsibilities for each one. Many times we are asked to serve on a committee but are completely unaware of its responsibilities and learn too late that we are unable to carry out the duties. A set of instructions for the sewing committee could read like this:

SEWING COMMITTEE DUTIES

The sewing committee will consist of a chairwoman, assistant chairwoman and _____ members. The committee will meet as often as necessary to carry out the following duties. All purchases and projects should be approved by the officers of the group.

1. Purchase materials and patterns (as instructed by officers). Your committee should consult the missionary about pattern, material and color preference whenever possible.
2. Hand out sewing to those who are willing to help. Prepare a list of all members of the group who are able to sew. Note whether they do difficult or plain sewing. Include the names of those who are unable to attend your meetings but can sew at home.
3. In a special notebook keep a record of the name, address and phone number of each woman who takes home a dress or article. Record the date the item is completed and returned to you. This will prevent accidental loss of material and patterns.

4. Keep a record of all work completed by your committee for the annual report.
5. If the missionary is home on furlough, you should arrange for her to be present at one of the meetings for fittings.
6. Keep a complete record of each missionary's measurements so that those who are sewing can refer to them in the absence of the missionary.
7. Check completed garments to make sure they are satisfactory in every detail.
8. Have an ironing board, iron and pressing cloth available. All garments should be pressed when finished.
9. Keep available a good supply of sharp scissors, thread, needles, buttons, snaps, zippers, etc.
10. Make sure sewing machines are in good running order for each meeting.
11. Have plenty of work ready for sewing or cutting at each meeting. Do not keep the women standing around waiting for something to do.
12. The chairwoman or assistant should arrive at the meeting early to have everything ready.
13. The chairwoman or the assistant chairwoman should be present at every meeting in order to instruct and answer questions.
14. If a commercial pattern is not available for articles such as drapes, towels, surgical drapes, etc., be sure to have detailed instructions typed or mimeographed, giving step-by-step procedures and completed sizes of finished articles.
15. Be sure to thank all who help you with the work.

After you have prepared a list of duties for each committee you need in your group, you will be ready to select prayerfully the women who will best be able to head each committee.

Copies of the duties for each committee should be filed along with the constitution in the secretary's records.

Each chairwoman should receive a copy of the duties for her committee and a copy of the group's constitution. These records should be kept in a notebook and passed on to the next chairwoman.

Not all committees work well. Most of us have attended committee meetings where coffee and chatter have occupied most of the time, and actual effort has been of little value. A well-organized, efficient committee complements the missionary group. A poorly organized, inefficient committee can cause confusion and trouble.

Try to imagine the problems that might have arisen if a committee had been in charge of building the ark. I suppose a portion of the progress report of the Noah's Ark Steering Committee chairman might have read as follows: "The pitch committee worked very efficiently and right on schedule until they arrived at the building site to water-proof the ark inside and out with pitch. They were frustrated to learn that construction on the ark had not started because the chairman of the Gopher Wood Committee had been called out of town on the day of his committee's meeting, and as a result the meeting was postponed. Several members of that committee are quite involved with other projects, but as soon as they can arrange another meeting, they will make plans to contact all gopher wood dealers for bids. The delay has also affected the ark building committee. Several members had to resign because they had planned to work during their vacations. . . ."

The tragedy of committee inefficiency is very evident in this little imaginary report. Mankind had an appointment with God's judgment. A flood was coming. There was no time for procrastination.

Many centuries have passed, but still there is no time for dillydallying. Judgment is coming. "And as it is appointed unto men once to die, but after this the judgment" (Heb. 9:27). Women's missionary group committees should be aware of the urgency of the Great Commission. We should make haste to be about the Master's business.

The chairwoman is an important part of any committee. A great deal of the committee's efficiency will depend on her planning. As soon as the committee has been appointed, the chairwoman should obtain the following information from the president or officers:

1. What is the committee expected to accomplish? What is its purpose?
2. What are the duties and responsibilities of the committee?
3. What deadlines have to be met?
4. What is the maximum budget allotted to the committee?
5. What are the duties of other committees?
6. What limitations in your group's constitution or bylaws affect your committee?
7. What traditions are important to the group? Change and new ideas should be encouraged, but you should avoid the complete overthrow of certain practices that have become important to the group; for example, the presentation of a corsage to the oldest lady present at each annual meeting.
8. Ask for any other information you may consider important to your committee.

The chairwoman should call each member to set the earliest possible date for the first meeting. When you have several weeks or months to work, you may be tempted to put off the meeting. Do not yield to the temptation—it will mean rushing and last-minute planning. Try to avoid it.

If the president is a member ex officio of all committees, as a courtesy, be sure to invite her to the meeting.

Well in advance of the first meeting, the committee members should be informed about the purpose of the committee. They should be asked to be prayerfully thinking about ideas and plans to present at the meeting. On more than one occasion I have gone to a committee meeting when everyone except the chairwoman was in complete ignorance of what was expected. It is difficult to pull ideas out of the air, and an embarrassing silence usually prevails when people are asked to do this. If the chairwoman is the only one prepared with ideas, it appears as though she is taking over the whole meeting.

Make an agenda or list of items for the committee to discuss. Leave room for suggestions from the other members. The chairwoman should preside at the meeting, making sure the discussion does not wander into a social vein. Present each item for discussion and dispose of it before proceeding further.

Fellowship is sweet. We all enjoy it. But it is the ruination of many committees! I am sure there would be a slump in the coffee business if committee meetings were suddenly abolished. I am not suggesting that it is wrong to serve refreshments or to chat, but fellowship should not be the primary reason for meeting. Inform the women that the meeting will begin promptly at 2:00 P.M. and will last for about an hour and a half (if you stick right to the business at hand), and that you will plan to serve coffee for those who can stay.

Appoint a secretary to keep notes at each meeting. Have her make a note of all suggestions and ideas. Discuss them thoroughly. No committee can utilize all the suggestions presented, so it will be necessary to pick the best of them. When the choice has been made, it is time for action. Many committees fail at this point. Discussion has not been difficult, but following through is another story. The chairwoman can avoid this pitfall if she assigns specific responsibilities to each member. Someone should keep a record of these assignments. Furthermore, the chairwoman should be responsible for checking to see if each lady is carrying out her assigned duty. A tactful chairwoman will be careful not to appear dictatorial. She will ask for volunteers or she will ask if someone is willing to do a certain task. Whenever a breakdown occurs in the implementation of the committee's work, steps should be taken immediately to correct the problem.

Avoid impulsive, spontaneous moves. Quite often an idea sounds good and is acted upon without consideration for the whole program. Afterward it becomes evident that the committee made a mistake that necessitates back-tracking and further action. Do not act before you think.

Keep the president and officers of your group informed of your committee's progress and plans. Always keep in mind that a committee is responsible to those who appoint it.

Keep a file of ideas and clippings that can be passed from chairwoman to chairwoman. Committees should keep written reports of their meetings and activities. A careful record of money spent should also be kept by the committee and a duplicate given to the group treasurer for reimbursement.

When a committee is called on to make a report to the group and that report contains recommendations that are not stated in the form of motions, they should be listed again at the end of the report so that action can be taken. After the reading of the report, a motion can be made to adopt the recommendations.

If the report ends with a resolution, the reporting member is supposed to move that the resolution be adopted. From that point on, the motion is handled like any other.

If the report contains no motions or recommendations, the presiding officer asks for a motion to accept the report.

13 Program Committee and Programming

It is difficult to outline the duties of the program committee, not because the duties are complicated but because it is the responsibility of the officers of a group to outline the work of its committees. I will list a few of the tasks that can be assigned to the program committee, but it will be up to each individual group to make the final decision.

1. Hold program committee meetings.
2. Plan the programs for a month at a time or for a year at a time according to the desires of your group.
3. Secure speakers and talent with the approval of the officers. Always remember that the program committee should keep in close consultation with the officers that appointed it. All committees are subordinate to the officers or executive committee.
4. Correspond with possible speakers, giving pertinent facts about the meeting.
5. Prepare programs if they are going to be needed. This may be the printed program for a specific meeting, or the program booklet that lists the meetings and committees for the year ahead.
6. Make sure microphones, screen and projector are available if needed.
7. If ushers are needed, this committee should secure them.
8. Make sure that offering plates are on hand.

9. Be sure that an announcement of the program reaches the officer who is responsible for its being put into the church bulletin.
10. Write thank-you notes to speakers and other special participants.
11. Keep an up-to-date file of good program ideas and suggestions for future reference. Pass this file on to the next committee.

The program committee should be aware of the proper etiquette of securing, entertaining and paying speakers. Extend your invitation as early as possible. Most missionaries, as well as other speakers, are busy with deputation meetings, and it will be necessary for them to work your meetings into their itineraries. If you use the telephone to secure a speaker, be sure to confirm the call by letter. Include the following information in your letter of invitation.

1. Give the date, time and place of meeting. Include a map or directions if the speaker is not familiar with the area.
2. Tell the type of meeting. (This helps the speaker to know how to dress. It is quite embarrassing to arrive at a come-as-you-are work meeting dressed for a banquet or vice versa.)
3. State the amount of time you are allotting to the speaker. At the time of the meeting, be sure to keep on schedule so that the speaker has the full amount of time allotted. Do not ask a missionary to show her slides and tell you all about her field of service and then give her twenty-five minutes in which to do it.
4. Include a note saying, "We will take care of your expenses." If your speaker is coming from out of the city, be sure to make arrangements for lunch or dinner. After a trip, she may want to freshen up a bit before being presented to the group. Be careful to

make this provision. Have someone on hand to greet the speaker at the door. Offer to help her carry her equipment. Do not let the speaker walk alone into a strange group. Assign someone to help her pick up her materials after the meeting. Make certain someone is with her at all times. It is easy to chat in private little groups and leave the guest speaker on the sideline.

Consider the cost of public transportation or automobile mileage when paying the speaker. If the distance is great, remember the meals that must be purchased en route. Add to this the honorarium that you feel is fair. Always consider the time that is consumed in preparation for your meeting, travel, and so on. Let us be fair to our Christian workers. If anyone is going to sacrifice, let it be the group that gave the invitation, not the speaker. Some groups are under the impression that mission boards pay the expenses of missionaries on deputation. This is not true.

PROGRAMMING HINTS

Some groups plan special meetings to attract new members. Others just drift along with the regular announcements of the regular meetings to be held in the regular place to do the regular things at the regular time. Needless to say, this will attract only the regular old faithfuls.

A little time and effort put into planning and preparation will make a big difference in your programming. "Plan the work and work the plan." A committee member or committee that learns the wisdom of detailed planning on paper and who then simply follows the steps indicated by that plan will produce well-organized meetings without haphazard, last-minute, hurry-scurry and wasted effort.

Plan early. If you are planning a year of meetings, be sure to include all available officers in your initial meetings so that you will be able to integrate their goals. Plan for a year of very special meetings that every woman in the church and Sunday School will want to attend. If you are planning meetings monthly or planning for several individual meetings during a year, be sure to do it with the same enthusiasm and diligence that you would muster if you were planning for a full year.

Almost all planning for the program committee will fall under four main categories: (1) decorations and theme; (2) program; (3) food; (4) publicity. Try to complete plans for one category at a time and then move on to the next. It is easy to get into a state of confusion if you try to handle all areas at one time. The following suggestions may help to stimulate thinking.

FOOD

Food is certainly not the most important reason for having a meeting, but it can be significant in the planning of a meeting. You must decide the type of meeting. Will it be a supper meeting, luncheon meeting or just an afternoon or evening meeting with dessert? Try to vary the type of meetings during a year. There are many ideas that will give variety to your program.

1. *Carry-in Supper or Luncheon*—You can call it a "Tote-in-Dinner."
2. *Planned Supper or Luncheon*—A committee can prepare the entire meal, and a freewill offering can be taken to cover the cost.
3. *Around-the-World Supper*—Serve foods from various countries: rice from Asia, coffee from Brazil, and so forth.
4. *Saladrama*—Serve all salads except for beverage and rolls: meat salads, fish salads, vegetable salads, potato salads, hot salads, cold salads, fruit salads and dessert salads.
5. *Dessert Smorgasbord*—The ladies eat at home and come at 7:00 or 7:15 P.M. to enjoy a variety of attractive desserts and coffee. This can also be

used for an afternoon meeting.

THEME AND DECORATIONS

Selecting a theme for your meeting is probably one of the most important decisions you will make. Almost all other phases of your planning will revolve around the theme.

1. *Around-the-World Theme*—Decorations can be from many continents or countries. The Around-the-World Supper suggestion can be used with this theme. In large gatherings, each table can be decorated to represent a different country or continent. In smaller groups, the committee can plan to carry out the theme in table centerpieces or backdrops.

2. *Special Country or Continent Theme*—Decorate the tables and room to represent the theme chosen. A decorating committee can do this for the entire group. You can use a centerpiece decoration for the speaker's table alone or for all the tables. An attractive backdrop behind the speaker's table can depict the theme. You can also use individual decorations for each place setting if you have an industrious committee. For an African theme, the committee can make centerpieces out of construction paper and straw to resemble African huts. Clothespin figures can be used for people. Empty coconut shells can also be used to make buildings. Attractive palm trees can be made from cardboard tubes wrapped in brown crepe paper with green construction paper leaves. You can borrow curios from missionaries.

3. *Slogan or Scripture Verse Theme*—Pick a Scripture verse or slogan for a theme and plan decorations around it. For example, you could choose "Go Ye into All the World." The world globe with flowers entwined can be used for a centerpiece on the speaker's table. Make a large stop-and-go signal

for the middle of the room and hang it from wires. Use a cardboard box to serve as the light. Paint a circle with flat red paint to represent the red light. Cut a circular hole below the red light and cover the opening with transparent green paper to represent the green light. A light bulb with a flasher button—available at hardware and variety stores—hanging inside will flash GO throughout the program.

PROGRAM

The program you plan should be interesting, inform-ing, inspiring and challenging. The musicians and speaker should be informed of the theme you choose. Here are a few program suggestions.

1. Good music—do not overlook the possibility of using some of the young people of your church.
2. Missionary speaker, if available.
3. Pastor's wife or lay speaker.
4. Missionary slides and films are available from our mission agencies. Write them for a list of titles.
5. Round-table discussions. Members of a missionary group, the pastor's wife or other women can par-ticipate. A good moderator should be selected to guide the discussion and to keep the speakers on time. Suggested topics are as follows:
   a. How can we vitalize our missionary vision?
   b. Are we putting too much emphasis on foreign missions? (The answer, of course, is that we cannot put too much emphasis on foreign mis-sions, but we can put too little on home mis-sions.)
   c. How effectively are we carrying out the Great Commission?

PUBLICITY

We often plan a tip-top program but put very little emphasis on the publicity and are disappointed when the

71

attendance is small. Beware of the mistake of thinking that everyone in the church is aware of your plans.

Appoint a committee to make posters for every available space in your church. Posters will take on added interest if you use something attractive as an eye-catcher. Add a bouquet under the words "Blossom Out for. . . ." Or use a toy telephone wired to poster board under the words "Calling All Women. . . ."

Announce the meeting in the church bulletin for several weeks. Make the announcement interesting. Send a letter to all the ladies in your group urging them to come and to bring someone as a guest. Make special announcements to be handed to every woman in the church and Sunday School. These announcements can be made out of construction paper. If your theme is "Go Ye into All the World," you can make the announcement in the form of the stop-and-go light.

Ask the men of the church to serve your supper. Everyone should know that it is "ladies' night out!"

The same special publicity methods can be used for your monthly meetings. Clever announcements will increase your attendance if you persist.

SPECIAL OCCASION MEETINGS

Take advantage of Easter and Mother's Day as opportunities to plan special meetings that will attract not only the ladies of the church but also their unsaved friends and relatives.

During the weeks preceding Easter, many women are very, very busy with housecleaning and spring sewing. They will welcome the idea of a pre-Easter breakfast as a time of relaxation and spiritual refreshment. Besides, this is an excellent occasion for spreading the gospel. Often we work feverishly on organization and projects, but we neglect to invite our unsaved friends and neighbors to come under the hearing of the gospel.

Keep the details of the meeting simple, but be sure to make it attractive. You can use paper plates, Styrofoam cups and pretty napkins. The centerpiece can be made with real or artificial spring flowers arranged around a cross, large Bible or open tomb with an angel sitting on a stone. These decorations can be made from cardboard or Styrofoam. If you have an especially ambitious committee, they can make an attractive bookmark for each lady who attends. The bookmark can be made from ribbon with a small gold cross painted on the front.

Some groups serve bacon and eggs or sausage and eggs along with juice, rolls and coffee. But this requires a great deal of work. I am suggesting that you serve fruit juice in three- or four-ounce paper cups. Place plates of sweet rolls on the table. Some of the ladies can bring coffee servers, and these can be filled and placed on the tables. This will eliminate the need for waitresses, and it will keep work to a bare minimum.

The program is the most important part of your meeting. Keep it short so that mothers can be home when their children arrive for lunch. Do not spend a lot of time making lengthy speeches and announcements, especially if there are visitors present. One or two musical numbers, a well-read Easter poem, the reading of the Scripture and a twenty-five or thirty minute talk is just about all you will need to plan. Be sure your speaker knows that you have a twofold purpose—reaching the unsaved with the gospel and bringing an Easter message of blessing to those who are Christians. Plan for a nursery so that mothers of young children can attend. Serve the younger children apart from their mothers so that unsaved women will be able to concentrate on the message.

The idea of the Easter breakfast is far more novel than the mother-daughter banquet idea. Yet I doubt if there is any other meeting during the year that has more possibilities for reaching the unsaved than the mother-daughter gathering. Unsaved daughters come because it is Mother's special day, and by the same token unsaved mothers are usually happy to be honored on this occasion. Almost without exception, when I speak at a mother-daughter program, I hear of a number of unsaved who are in attendance because a praying mother or daughter is using the meeting as an opportunity for reaching her unsaved loved one. Often someone in a backslidden condition returns to the Lord. Young girls in the junior high department and above should be urged to bring their mothers to the program, especially if they are unsaved. Some of the women should be assigned to make certain the visitors are made to feel welcome throughout the evening. Be sure that some little Sunday School girl is not left alone in a corner with her mother who may not be acquainted with anyone at the banquet.

Businessmen have found it is profitable to use the "come-on" type of advertising to bring potential customers into their stores. As Christians, we should be just as alert and clever in bringing the unsaved within the hearing of the gospel. No group should plan a mother-daughter program without being as diligent in prayer as it would be for a series of evangelistic meetings.

Your mother-daughter affair can take several forms. The banquet is the most common. You can have the meal prepared and divide the cost per person, or you can have a planned carry-in type menu. I prefer the latter because very often a mother has several daughters and the cost of a prepared meal is prohibitive. Try to make it possible for everyone to attend.

If you do not want to have a banquet, you can have your program first and plan a dessert smorgasbord afterwards. This plan works well especially for small churches.

The program is the important part of your evening. You will need a mistress of ceremonies who will be very careful that the stories and jokes are not so personal as to be offensive. The time allowed for this should be limited. The toast to mothers and the toast to daughters are almost traditions. You can have a skit or humorous reading, but be careful about using both. You will also have special musical numbers and a speaker. This will add up to a big evening. You will have to be careful that the program is not too long. Several years ago I spoke at a mother-daughter banquet that had so much on the program that the preliminaries were not over until five minutes after ten. By that time, nearly everyone past forty-five was dozing, and all the mothers of young children were trying to keep them from open rebellion. This is much too late for a speaker to put across a message. Do not try to do everything at one banquet.

Consider using the girls in the junior or junior high departments for special music. They can sing a medley of choruses or familiar hymns. This will attract their mothers if they do not attend church.

Ask the men of the church to serve as waiters so that the ladies can be free to enjoy their night. Many groups present a plant or gift to the oldest lady or to the mother with the most daughters. It is nice to make the presentation, but you should change the qualifier each year because the same ladies may win each time.

Consider limiting the age of the children attending. On a number of occasions I have spoken to a group with several small babies and a large group of preschoolers sitting unattended in the front row. One mother of several boys proudly arrived with a nine-day-old daughter. I appreciated the mother's delight, but the baby had not yet learned how to behave at a banquet, and she carried on her own program throughout the evening. It is very difficult to speak with this kind of competition, but it is more difficult to hear. Remember, this banquet may be the only time that some mothers will hear the gospel. If younger children come to the banquet, plan a special program for them during the speaking part of the meeting.

The program committee will be called on not more than two or three times a year to plan a special meeting. These meetings can be a great blessing to all who attend if the committee does a good job.

14 *Project Committee*

The project committee is one of the most important committees in a women's missionary group. If this committee does not plan well and operate efficiently, the entire group will be at loose ends. Nothing will be accomplished, and there will be no purpose for the group's existence.

We waste a great deal of time and effort in our groups when we fail to plan well into the future for our projects. Many women's organizations are lax in the area of projected planning. Committees are often so busy completing present projects that they do not think about the work to be done in the future; then suddenly the chairwoman realizes that there will be no work for the next month's meeting, and she sends an SOS to a nearby missionary or an agency, hoping that she can secure some kind of project that can be worked on until she writes to the church's missionaries. Instead of working on the *needs* of their missionaries, they work on a project to help keep the members of the group busy.

Many women's missionary organizations appoint one woman or one committee to take full responsibility for all projects, including sewing, quilting, handwork and white cross. In addition, they usually have to purchase all materials and sewing supplies, make provision for sewing machines and correspond with the missionaries to learn of their needs. This is too much for one person or even for one committee.

Dividing the responsibilities would greatly increase a

group's accomplishment and smoothness of operation. Instead of expecting one committee to do all the work relating to projects, consider the appointment of a planning committee with one of the officers as the chairwoman. This would free the project committee to concentrate on the completion of work already assumed by the group. When a project is finished, the planning committee could inform them of the next task.

The planning committee should meet periodically during the year. This committee should correspond with the missionaries of the church to secure a list of ideas for projects. A detailed file or notebook should be started and a record kept of every letter sent by the committee or received from the missionary. All correspondence should be dated and the lists of all needs should be prepared in duplicate. Place the first copy in the notebook or file and give the second copy to the officers. When the group votes to accept responsibility for all or part of the needs, this should be recorded for future reference. The planning committee should then prepare a copy of the items to be made or purchased, including the name of the missionary, size, pattern choice, color preference, suggested materials, quantity and deadline date. The project committee receives the copy and immediately proceeds to work out details for accomplishing the assignment. This procedure prevents the loss of time between projects; the group always has a waiting list of projects ready to work on.

In most groups, committees are appointed either annually or biannually when the new officers are elected. A month or two before the end of a term, the officers and committees begin to wind up their work. Then the election takes place, and the work comes to a standstill until the new committees are appointed and activated. Much valuable time slips by before the new committee can write to the missionaries and receive answers. To avoid this problem, rotate your committees. Instead of appointing completely new committees after each election, add one or two new members to replace the one or two who automatically retire. The rotating committee never stops working. This system is especially helpful for both the planning and project committees. It is invaluable to new officers coming into the organization. It eliminates the necessity of starting from the ground up to reorganize after every election. In addition, it is an excellent way to train new workers.

Another problem area for many groups is the matter of time. How can a group conduct a business meeting, have a devotional time, spend ample time in prayer, enjoy a fellowship period and still have sufficient time for the project committee to conduct a profitable work session, especially at an evening meeting?

It would be nice if I could produce an ideal outline to guarantee a successful program in all of these areas. It is impossible, however, because missionary groups, like dresses, must be tailored to fit. Darts, tucks and adjustments to lengthen and shorten are all necessary to make a stock pattern fit perfectly. The program that works well in one church may be cumbersome in another. It is important for each group to spend time analyzing goals and needs so that they can get the most value out of the time allotted for monthly meetings.

Older ladies with diminished family demands may be able to meet two or three times a month for daytime meetings, but younger mothers or working women may find that they can spend only one evening a month away from home and responsibilities. Daytime meetings are out of the realm of possibility for them. Others can attend meetings in the daytime but are unable to be away from home in the evening. Still others are unable to attend meetings at any time, but are willing to sew or work at home. If a church has several groups, these ladies can choose the meeting time that best suits their schedules. When a church has just one group, all of these problems must be considered.

For years I was a member of an evening group. We accomplished a great deal and supplied large quantities of clothing and other articles for our missionaries. Instead of appointing one project chairwoman to direct all of the work activities for the entire group, we appointed chairwomen for the following committees: quilting; white cross; handwork (flannelgraph, wordless books, bookmarks and the like); used clothing; greeting cards; knitting; rag rugs and sewing. Each committee had a chairwoman who was responsible for seeing that supplies were on hand and work laid out before the meeting started. Every committee was given a detailed order sheet stating the quantity and type of items that were needed for the missionary. The completion date was also put on the order sheet. If the committee was unable to finish the work at regular meetings, the chairwoman would call her workers together for a special work meeting during the month or would ask some of the women to take work home for completion.

Devotions consisted of a short Scripture passage and either a missionary poem or thought for the day at the beginning of the business meeting. (Business meetings can and should be short if the officers meet to discuss the business before it is presented to the group.) The women worked quietly during the business time but stopped for the prayer time. One meeting a year was set aside for a fellowship supper at which time a missionary speaker was invited to challenge the women. During regular meetings, the women often listened to information about missionaries and mission fields while they worked.

Other groups have an evening meeting and one or two work meetings a month for women who can attend during the day. You will have to adjust these suggestions to your organization. Let the women decide how they want to carry on their work projects. Some, no doubt, will want to attend special workdays while others will prefer to work at home. If they attend the regular monthly meeting, it should make little difference how they complete their projects.

Sometimes we try to do too much in one meeting. Many groups have become ineffective because they have taken ideas from other groups and utilized them without considering the effect the new plan will have on the existing program. For instance, a group that is organized primarily as a work meeting with a prayer time and a short business meeting hears about a sister organization that has received a great blessing by spending thirty minutes studying "Missions in the Early Church." This group also learned about another group that developed a missionary quiz so that the members could become better acquainted with the missionaries supported by their church. They added these new features to their regular monthly meeting. The result? Too little time to work on projects for the missionaries.

Unfortunately, it is possible to have a great deal of activity with little or no accomplishment. In order to prevent a cluttered program or agenda, each group should take a periodic objective look at the meetings. Begin with the constitution. What is the stated purpose of the group? (Every group should have a constitution which states its purpose. It will act as a mooring over the years to keep the organization in line with its original intent.)

If your purpose is prayer and work meetings, hold the business and devotions to a minimum. If your purpose is fellowship and study, the work projects should be kept to a minimum. Logic tells us that we cannot have a half-hour devotional program, a half hour for missionary letters and information, ample prayer time, a lengthy business meeting and refreshments—and still have time for a productive work meeting. Something must be eliminated.

15 *Project Order Form*

NAME OF MISSIONARY OR MISSIONARY FAMILY

CLOTHING SIZES

	Dress or Suit	Shoes	Hose	Coat	Hat
Husband	_____	____	____	____	____
Wife	_____	____	____	____	____
Children					
1.	_____	____	____	____	____
2.	_____	____	____	____	____
3.	_____	____	____	____	____
4.	_____	____	____	____	____

COLOR PREFERENCES

Husband	_____	____	____	____	____
Wife	_____	____	____	____	____
Children					
1.	_____	____	____	____	____
2.	_____	____	____	____	____
3.	_____	____	____	____	____
4.	_____	____	____	____	____

MATERIAL PREFERENCES

Climatic Conditions _____

Winter _____

Spring _____

Summer _____

Fall _____

Laundering or dry cleaning conditions _____
Best type of material to use in garments _____

_____

STYLE PREFERENCES

List style preferences, such as sleeve length, dress length, nightwear styles, etc.

Husband _____

Wife _____

Children

1. _____

2. _____

3. _____

4. _____

HOBBIES AND INTERESTS

List secular magazines, Christian magazines, books, taped music, crafts, sewing, etc.

Husband _____
_____

Wife _____
_____

Children

1. _____
_____

2. _____
_____

3. _____
_____

4. _____
_____

HOUSEHOLD NEEDS

Room	Room Size	Windows	Color	Bed Size
Living Room	_____	_____	_____	_____
Dining Room	_____	_____	_____	_____
Kitchen	_____	_____	_____	_____
Bedroom 1	_____	_____	_____	_____

Bedroom 2 _____ _____ _____ _____
Bedroom 3 _____ _____ _____ _____
Office _____ _____ _____ _____
Other _____ _____ _____ _____

SHOPPING FACILITIES

Describe shopping facilities. How far from your home? How large is the selection you have to choose from? How expensive is it to shop for clothing and household needs?

_____

_____

_____

MAILING AND CUSTOMS' REGULATIONS

Instructions for wrapping and package size _____

_____

Customs' information, including proper labels_____

_____

Articles not to be sent to field _____

_____

MAILING ADDRESS

_____

_____

_____

MONEY GIFTS

Give instructions for sending checks, money orders, gift money, etc. _____

_____

ITEMS YOU WOULD LIKE TO RECEIVE
PERIODICALLY DURING TERM

____ 1. Jell-O   ____ 6. Clothing
____ 2. Cake mix   ____ 7. Condiments
____ 3. Hose   ____ 8. Confections
____ 4. Toiletry items ____ 9. Bed linens
____ 5. Cosmetic items ____10. Bath towels

____11. Kitchen linens   ____28.
____12. Office supplies   ____29.
____13. Construction   ____30.
       paper   ____31.
____14. Tools   ____32.
____15. Gummed stars   ____33..
       and seals   ____34.
____16.   ____35.
____17.   ____36.
____18.   ____37.
____19..   ____38.
____20.   ____39.
____21.   ____40.
____22.   ____41.
____23.   ____42.
____24.   ____43.
____25.   ____44.
____26.   ____45.
____27.

If it is possible to send Green Label packages to your field, give instructions, including information about the Green Label customs' stamp that permits packages under two pounds to reach you duty free.

16 *Requisition Form*

The question that is asked most often by women's groups is, "What can we do? How can we find out about the needs of missionaries?" Most of the groups seem to be rolling bandages. Somehow the thought of missionaries and rolled bandages seems inseparable. All missionaries have needs, but some of them do not need bandages. They are not doing medical work. One missionary told me that they received a large supply of rolled bandages, which they sewed together to make sheets. I imagine you are chuckling. We rip the sheets apart and they sew them back together.

How can we overcome this waste of time and effort? I have spoken to women's groups that have complained that they have sent letters to their missionaries requesting a list of needs, and often no list is forthcoming. Why? I believe it is because of a communication gap between the groups and the missionary. Most of us have been embarrassed at one time or another because a friend has said, "I want to get you a present. What do you need?" The first thought that goes through our minds is, "I wonder how much they want to spend?" When we ask missionaries for a list of their needs, they no doubt feel much the same way. They are not sure whether we are referring to new clothes, flannelgraph sets, a station wagon or rolled bandages.

A missionary shared her concern with me in a letter. She said, "During the first few months of each year, we receive letters from several women's groups asking what their groups can send us during the year to come. We appreciate their desire to help—but in composing our answer we must consider several questions. What are the abilities of this group (in regard to sewing projects, etc.) and how much can they spend? What do we need? We do not want them to spend time and money making something that cannot be used. On the other hand, it must be something that we can get along without if they decide not to send it. If it is something we need urgently, we may try to order it ourselves. If a group writes in February, it will no doubt be April before they receive the answer because the mails are slow. By that time the group is working on several other projects; so they do not fill our request until the late fall. We do not receive the package until the following May or June. It would be a big help if the group would notify the missionary that they plan to assume the project. This would give the missionary the opportunity of giving the need to another group if it is not accepted.

I hope that I have not sounded too critical of the women and the work they are doing, as we certainly are thankful for all they do, and we have had wonderful fellowship with the various groups when we have been home."

I suggest the use of a REQUISITION FORM to aid your group in securing project ideas from missionaries. Such a form can be designed to suit the needs of your group. If none of the ladies in your church knit, you can eliminate knitted items from the list and substitute something your group can provide.

This form has been used to great advantage by both missionaries and missionary groups. One missionary said that it helped to stimulate her thinking when she received it so that she could more quickly make a list of needs. Use this form to send to the missionary on the field so that she can fill it out and return it to you. If you mail items to the field, it would be wise for you to inquire about the duty that must be paid for packages received in that country. Perhaps your group can send that amount of money to the mission board to be added to the missionary's account.

Some groups work very efficiently to prepare all the items that a missionary needs during furlough time. These items are packed in barrels and are shipped to the field with all of the other belongings of the missionary. When the missionary is at home, it is wise to sit down and go over the list. Many missionaries are reluctant to tell their needs for fear that they will be criticized for asking too much. Many times a missionary puts down just a few items when the needs are greater. Assure the missionaries of your group's desire to do more because of your interest in the work they are doing.

When you use the REQUISITION FORM, you can be sure that you will not be wasting your time making items that are not needed. Too many groups make items hoping that a missionary can use them, rather than working on actual needs.

SAMPLE REQUISITION FORM

Our Ladies' Missionary Group would like to help supply some of your personal needs or needs on your field. Please indicate on this list the items you can use and note the quantity.

_____	Wordless books	_____	Luncheon cloths
_____	Bookmarks	_____	Luncheon napkins
_____	Mounted pictures	_____	Baby bibs
_____	Pill envelopes	_____	Layettes
	Greeting cards	_____	Pajamas
_____	(Plain)	_____	Nightgowns
_____	(Mounted)	_____	Bathrobes
_____	(Scripture)	_____	Dish towels
_____	(Notepaper)	_____	Dresses
_____	Beanbags	_____	Shirts (boys')
_____	Stuffed toys	_____	Shorts (boys' boxer)
_____	Pot holders	_____	Blouses
_____	Aprons	_____	Skirts
_____	Doilies	_____	Slippers
_____	Sheets	_____	Laundry bags
_____	Pillowcases	_____	Turkish towels

Requisition Form

_____	Washcloths		Wrappers
_____	Huck towels	_____	(18" x 18")
_____	Sweaters	_____	(36" x 36")
_____	Mittens	_____	(Glove wrappers)
_____	Afghans	_____	Scrub suits
_____	Rag rugs	_____	Scrub gowns
_____	Flannelgraph sets	_____	Surgical caps
_____	Flannelgraph back-	_____	Surgical masks
	grounds	_____	Surgical sheets
	Rolled bandages	_____	Surgical drapes
_____	1" x 10'	_____	Mayo stand cover
_____	2" x 10'	_____	Abdominal packs
_____	3" x 10'	_____	Hot water bottle
	Gauze squares		covers
_____	2" x 2"	_____	Drawsheets
_____	4" x 4"	_____	Bedpan covers
	Sheeting squares	_____	Knit Ace bandages
_____	2" x 2"	_____	Q-Tips
_____	3" x 3"	_____	Window drapes
_____	4" x 4"	_____	Bedspreads
_____	Cotton balls		Quilts
_____	Baby sacques	_____	(Heavy)
_____	Hospital gowns	_____	(Medium)
	Binders	_____	(Light)
_____	(T binders)	_____	Pencils
_____	(Abdominal	_____	Crayons
	binders)	_____	Pencil carriers
_____	(Double T)	_____	Pins
_____	(Breast)	_____	Thread
		_____	Needles
		_____	Empty bottles

Other information not listed:

Wearing apparel—Please indicate size, color, material, style or pattern preference.

Flannelgraph—Please list title preferred and type of background.

Quilts—Please state size: king, queen, full, twin or crib.

Greeting cards—If you want cards stamped with Scripture verses, please include a copy of the verse or verses in the national language so we can have a rubber stamp made.

Please include packaging and mailing instructions.

17 *Personal Measurement Chart*

The sewing chairwoman should make sure that a personal measurement chart is filled out for every member of a missionary family. This information will be of great help to anyone sewing for a missionary. After the missionary has gone to the field, the group can refer to this chart whenever work is done for the family. It will save much time that will otherwise be spent trying to get this information by correspondence. Each missionary should have copies of this chart so that the group at home can be notified when sizes change. When the missionary notifies the group of a change, it should be recorded neatly on the chart so that the measurements are kept up-to-date.

The master copy of the Personal Measurement Chart should always remain in the group's file with duplicate copies to be made for the person sewing the garment.

NAME OF MISSIONARY _____
AGE OF CHILD _____
COLORING _____ SKIN _____
HAIR _____ EYES _____

The following measurements are needed so that patterns can be adjusted to correct size.
BUST SIZE   _____ inches
   (measure over fullest part, slightly higher in back)
BACK WIDTH   _____ inches
   (underarm to underarm)

Personal Measurement Chart

WAIST   _____inches
   (hold the tape snug and measure the entire waist)
HIP   _____inches
   (measure over the fullest part, about 7" below waist)
BACK HIP   _____inches
   (measure over the fullest part, side to side)
FRONT CHEST   _____inches
   (measure armhole to armhole, 3" below neck)
BACK WIDTH   _____inches
   (measure armhole to armhole, 4" below neck)
WAIST LENGTH FRONT   _____inches
   (measure from neck to waist)
WAIST LENGTH BACK   _____inches
   (measure from neck to waist)
WAIST LENGTH SIDE   _____inches
   (measure from center shoulder to waist for both sides)
UNDERARM WAIST LENGTH _____inches
   (measure 1" below armpit to waist)
SKIRT LENGTH FRONT   _____inches
   (measure from waist to hem)
SKIRT LENGTH BACK   _____inches
   (measure from waist to hem)
SHOULDER   _____inches
   (measure from base of neck to arm socket)
UPPER SLEEVE LENGTH   _____inches
   (measure from shoulder to elbow with arm bent)
LOWER SLEEVE LENGTH   _____inches
   (measure from elbow to wrist)
UNDERARM SLEEVE LENGTH _____inches
   (measure from armpit to wrist, with arm straight)

18 Missionary Treasure Chest or Cupboard

"Would you like to visit our treasure chest and take some things that you can use?" Missionaries love to receive this invitation because they can gather so many needed items to put into waiting barrels. Most groups have a missionary chest of some type. It may be a large sturdy box, an old trunk, a cupboard, a real honest-to-goodness chest made by men of the church or even a room complete with shelves, drawers, rods for hanging garments and a mirror to check the fit of garments.

Some groups fill their chests at periodic "treasure chest showers." Others open the chest at every meeting so the ladies can bring items that they have purchased at a sale, sewed, knitted or handcrafted for the church missionaries. Keep the chest full and neatly and attractively arranged. When a missionary visits the church or speaks to the group, you can open the chest and invite the missionaries to take a supply of needed articles. Treasure chest items should be given as gifts to the missionary speaker in addition to, and not in place of, a monetary honorarium.

Keep the ladies informed about items that are needed for the cupboard. Because we are giving "gifts" from this chest to our beloved missionaries, we should not put used items in it. Used items can be kept in a separate place. Missionaries do not mind receiving seasonal items they can use while on furlough, but the treasure chest should be filled with brand spanking new things. If the ladies of the church are excited about the treasure chest project, you will have plenty of a variety of good articles available; and you will not have to be stingy or worry that the missionary will take too much. Remember, a four-year term is a long time, and we should urge the missionaries to take all they need and can use. I have been in treasure chest rooms where large, expensive articles are side by side with pot holders, dish cloths and sewing kits. Floral bedsheet sets are next to a stack of dish cloths. An electric blanket is side by side with an assortment of wooden spoons. All of these things are important, but the missionary may feel uncomfortable about choosing between the larger and the smaller items and will probably settle for a few small things rather than appear to be greedy. To overcome this, divide your treasure closet into sections. Put all the large things in one area and the smaller ones in another place. Take the missionary to the larger gifts first and let her choose several of them. Then go to the other section and get what she needs. It is nice to have a section of freebies for children so they can select a few things.

Keep a supply of shopping bags and boxes on hand. Decorate them and include the name of your church and group on them. These containers will not only provide a means of transporting treasures, but will help the missionaries when they write "thank you" notes at the end of a speaking tour and find your church name on the bags. Some groups are allowing the treasure chest to squeeze out all other projects. We still need sewing groups and REQUISITION FORMS (see chapter 16) to provide needed garments to meet certain specifications of size, type and color to suit the missionary. Keep sewing machines humming, the scissors cutting, knitting needles clicking, bandages rolling and fingers flying. There is so much to do and so little time to do it if we are going to supply our missionaries' needs and prepare them to go into all the world to preach the gospel.

If you have had your missionary cupboard for years, it is no doubt time to make some changes. Get rid of old items no one has taken. Rearrange the shelves. Add some new items. The following list of ideas may help you whether you are adding to the old treasure chest or starting a new one for the first time:

APPLIANCES
Can openers—electric and
   hand-operated
Electric irons
Electric mixers
Fans—electric and hand
Ice cream freezers—hand-
   operated
Meat grinders—hand-operated
Toasters

CLOTHING AND PERSONAL
ITEMS
Children's hose
Clothes brushes
Facial tissues
Footlets
Garment bags
Gloves—men's and women's
Handbags for ladies
Handkerchiefs
Jewelry
Layette items
Men's belts
Men's socks
Mittens
Panty hose
Regular hose
Sandals, slippers, thongs
Scarves
Shoe bags
Shoeshine kits and polish
Ties and tie clasps
Tote bags
Umbrellas
Wallets
Watches
Women's belts

COSMETICS
After-shave and colognes for
   men
Barrettes
Bath oils
Bobby pins
Combs
Curlers
Deodorants
Emery boards and files for nails
Hairbrushes
Hair clips
Hair conditioners
Hairnets
Hair-setting lotions
Hair sprays
Hand creams
Moisturizers
Perfumes for women
Shampoos
Soaps—bar, liquid
Talc for men and women
Toothbrushes
Toothpaste

DECORATIVE ITEMS
Baskets
Candleholders and candles
Doilies and scarves
Figurines
Florist clay
Mirrors—large and small
Picture frames
Picture hangers—including
   some for cement walls
Pictures—variety for framing
Seasonal decorations
Sofa pillows

Vases

GAMES
Coloring books
Games
Paint-by-number pictures
Puzzles

HOUSE AND YARD ITEMS
Batteries—all sizes
Enamel paint
Garden hoses
How-to-do-it magazines
Insect bombs
Insect repellents
Latex house paint
Mediums for paints
Paintbrushes
Paint removers
Paint rollers
Paint thinners
Plant fertilizers
Spray paints—gold,
    aluminum, silver
Tools
Vegetable and flower seeds
Watering cans

HOUSEHOLD ITEMS
Cleansers
Clocks
Clotheslines—rope, plastic
Clothespins—wood, plastic
Con-Tac paper
Curtains
Dust mops
Feather dusters
Flashlights
Household brushes
Ironing boards
Ironing board pad and covers
Laundry bags
Plastic-coated wire hangers

Rag rugs
Scrub pails
Shelf paper
Soap trays
Sponges
Washboards

KITCHEN ITEMS
Aluminum bread pans, pie
    pans, muffin tins, cookie
    sheets, etc.
Aprons
Cutlery
Dishes
Hot pads
Metal teapots
Measuring cups
Mixing and measuring spoons
Oven mitts
Plastic bags all sizes—sand-
    wich, lawn, etc.
Place mats
Plastic knives, forks and spoons
Plastic tumblers
Pots and pans
Pot holders
Recipes *(those not containing
    concentrates and prepared
    items that are hard to get on
    the field)*
Silverware
Teakettles—large and small
Thermal glasses and pitchers
Thermos bottles
Trivets
Tupperware

LINEN ITEMS
Bath mats
Bath towels
Bed pads
Bed pillows
Blanket bags

Dishcloths
Dish towels
Hand towels
Mattress covers
Napkins
Paper napkins
Pillowcases
Quilts
Sheet blankets
Sheets
Shower curtains and hooks
Spreads
Tablecloths
Thermal blankets
Washcloths

MUSICAL ITEMS
Hymnals
Musical instruments—harmonicas, rhythm instruments, recorders, etc.
Special songbooks

OFFICE SUPPLIES
Acrylic paints
Ball-point pens and refills
Binoculars
Construction paper
Dictionaries
Erasers—pencil, typewriter
Felt-tip markers—black and colored
Flashbulbs or cubes
Gift wrapping, ribbon and bows
Greeting cards
Index cards
Notebook paper—lined, plain
Notebooks—bound and spiral
Notepaper
Oil paints
Paper punches
Pencils
Poster paints

Rubber cement, glue—Elmer's, epoxy
Staple removers
Staplers and staples
Stationery
Stencil and stylus kits for mimeograph
Tapes—cassette and reel *(blank and recorded)*
Tapes—mending, transparent, masking, correction
Typewriter ribbons
Typing paper
Watercolors
World atlas

SEWING ITEMS
Bias tape
Buttons
Elastic
Hooks and eyes
Laces and trims
Mending tapes
Needles
Razor blades
Rickrack
Safety pins
Scissors
Snaps
Thread
Yard goods—enough for dress
Zippers

TEACHING HELPS
Award items
Bible maps and charts
Books for children and adults
Chalk
Crayons
Flannelgraph boards
Flannelgraph sets
Hand puppets
Illustrated Bible stories

Illustrated songs	Scrapbooks
Letter sets and stencils	Seals—star, animal, flower
Marionettes	

The tool selection of the treasure chest can be a special project of the men of a church. Most missionaries need saws, hammers, crescent wrenches, etc., for their service on the field. Men could fill this need through their classes or missionary organization. If each man would give one dollar a month, there could be twenty-five or thirty dollars in a fund to purchase tools. The passing missionary can browse through the chest and take a few as needed. While missionaries are on the field, tools are lost, broken or stolen and must be replaced. A missionary told me that replacing tools almost always comes last, if at all. They are used almost daily. Single girls also need a certain number of tools.

This is an excellent idea, not only for men's groups but for women's groups as well (provided the ladies consult the men about the best tools to buy). I always thought that a saw was a saw until my husband caught me cutting off a tree branch with a saw that saws metal and not wood. After I finished with it, it was good for neither metal nor wood!

I doubt that men are too enthusiastic about our supply cupboards when they are filled with sheets, towels and pillowcases. Perhaps you could clear off a shelf and reserve it for tools. Have a tool shower at one of your meetings, inviting the men to this once-a-year event. If the men become sufficiently interested in the project, they may build a large chest for tools; or, better yet, they may even decide to make it their own project.

Members of the church can make out certificates offering their services. For example: a meal for an individual or family; free lodging; a homemade cake or pie; a day at the cottage as a guest of the family; use of a cottage or cabin for a few days or a week; a day of swimming at a member's pool; a day of waterskiing or fishing (including use of equipment); a day at the zoo (including a picnic lunch); a tune-up for the missionary's car; free service on a radio; free dry cleaning (dress or suit); a shampoo and set; a haircut; free mending; baby-sitting for missionaries' children. These certificates can be as varied as the talents and occupations of the members of your church.

Innovate—try to make your treasure chest or supply cupboard different from any others. This will make it possible for the missionary to secure a larger variety of the items needed on the field. Keep an accurate record of all the items that are stored and all the items that are taken, including the name of the missionary.

19 Project Suggestions for Women's Groups

Ask your missionary before starting any project. Duty is prohibitive in some countries. We must guard against causing hardship by sending materials that have not been requested.

Before mailing things overseas, check carefully. For example, missionaries in Liberia were advised by their field council to tell folks at home NOT to mail Green Label parcels to that country because of the high incidence of robbery. Very few of those parcels were reaching those to whom they were sent. Such situations may change from time to time; so it is best to contact the missionary before mailing.

1. Offer to reproduce Bible verses in the language of the country where your missionary works. This can save much time on the mission field. One missionary reported that these verses are really prized by children who attend her classes. The group can also put these verses in booklets and tie them with colorful yarn. Pictures from Sunday School papers can be added.

2. Type and mail out a missionary's prayer letter. This could save hours of time; and if your group can also take care of the postage, the missionary would be greatly helped.

3. Subscribe to the *Baptist Bulletin* for your missionaries who do not receive it. Contact the *Baptist Bulletin*, 1300 North Meacham Road,

Schaumburg, Illinois 60173–4888 for current foreign subscription rates.

4. Most missionaries have tape players or cassettes. Tape special programs presented in your church: sermons, singing and so forth. They also like to receive classical, martial and sacred music on tape. Be sure to check the speed of their recorder so that they can play it on their equipment.

5. Consult your missionaries to learn if you may provide gifts for them to share on their fields. Their friends have birthdays both on the field and at home. They like to share Christmas gifts too. Ask for suggestions, then watch for sales and choose good quality items that you would not be ashamed to give your friends. Be sure to include various kinds of gift wrap, ribbon and bows in the assortment of gifts. *Give these items to the missionaries before they return to the field so that the things can be packed in the barrels. If you mail them, the missionary will have to pay duty on each package.*

6. Buy Christmas merchandise in the AFTER CHRISTMAS SALES. Put some in your missionary chest. Your ladies could have fun decorating the satin-covered balls with old beads, sequins, rickrack and ribbon. Missionaries enjoy these for their homes, for a schoolroom or for an extra pretty gift for another missionary.

7. Remember the missionaries (men too) on their birthdays with a greeting card and note. Cards sent at Valentine's Day, Easter, Thanksgiving, Christmas and on anniversaries are very much appreciated. All the ladies in the group could sign the cards. *Cards for foreign missionaries should be sent airmail so they arrive on time.*

8. Plan a "Welcome Home Shower" for the missionary family who is newly arrived in the States.

Gifts of food (nonperishable) are always welcome. Other ideas: pre-moistened towelettes, shoe polish pads, an up-to-date road atlas, personal clothing, household items, games and books for children. Make this a special time with a program and social hour. Do not forget that money is always a help. You might have a money tree as a centerpiece for the serving table.

9. Both home and foreign missionaries like subscriptions to specific periodicals.

10. Missionaries love to receive food items, such as cake mixes, dried fruit, candy, Jell-O, whipped topping, chocolate chips, powdered sugar, brown sugar and other dry mixes that are unavailable or expensive on the field. One group puts these items in tin cans and seals them airtight.

11. Enroll your missionary children in Christian book clubs and pay the subscription cost for a given number of books a year.

12. Adopt a child at one of the children's homes. The homes will give you a list of items you can provide for the child.

13. A missionary might like to have a rubber stamp made of certain Bible verses in a national language (one verse per stamp). Also rubber stamps with return addresses or dates may be welcome. Be sure to include ink and pad. These are available wherever rubber stamps are made. Secure the verse from the missionary and be very careful that all the accent marks, and so forth, are correct.

14. Send home missionaries a book of postage stamps from time to time.

15. Make felt greeting cards in the shapes of trees, bells, candles, and other holiday shapes and trim with glitter. The missionary would enjoy a box of these to send to his special friends and to

his family in the states.

16. Fill egg-shaped hosiery containers with little trinkets and toys to send to missionary children. You might fill them with beads for the ladies and sewing notions for the missionaries' sewing supply cupboards. You also might leave the hose in the container and send it. If you decorate the outside of the egg, it can be used as a Christmas tree ornament to be given as an award.

17. Make nylon scrubbers for the missionary cupboard and send a few along to the missionary on the field from time to time.

18. Paint designs on dish towels and aprons with liquid embroidery. The cheery colors will certainly brighten the kitchen for the missionary.

19. Make felt beanies and decorate them to be used by the missionary for awards.

20. Make pencil holder awards. Cut two pieces of felt in desired shape (bell, animals). Decorate with sequins, metallic braid, contrasting felt or liquid embroidery. Glue together, leaving space for a pencil to be inserted. Missionaries use these for awards.

21. Make packets of beads. Include string so that the missionary can use them in craft classes to attract students.

22. Make decoupage pictures. Have someone show ladies in your group how to make them so that they can be put in the missionary chest or sent as gifts to missionaries.

23. Make plaques from plaster of paris. These are especially good for awards for home missionaries and the Sunday School and VBS in the home church.

24. Ladies who have learned the art of ceramics can contribute many items to the missionary treasure chest, such as casseroles, salt-and-pepper

shakers, vases, figurines and similar items.

25. Do you know a secretary? Ask her to save pieces of paper she otherwise would throw away. File cards can also be used. Make memory verse cards or picture cards for the missionary to use as awards. The paper can be cut into uniform size to be used for stationery. It can be decorated with flowers and pictures from greeting cards.

26. Cover wire hangers with small nylon bows made from net. They can also be covered with plastic or encased in yarn. This is helpful in a humid climate where wire hangers rust.

27. Make tote bags of sturdy cloth (upholstery squares are good), 18" x 36". Fold in half. Hem ends and sew side seams. Lace a drawstring through hemmed ends. Put a design or missionary's name on the outside with embroidery or liquid embroidery. These can also be made in quantity for the missionary to use as awards.

28. Make layettes for the missionary to use as a gift for new mothers. Include four diapers, a sacque, gown, wrapping blanket (one yard square), safety pins. Tie in bundle.

29. Make foam place mats. Cut Art Foam into place mat size. Use a light coating of glue to fasten pictures from greeting cards, magazines, etc., to the foam material. Cover with clear Con-Tac paper and stitch with the machine around edges.

30. Cut animals and fruit shapes from Art Foam and decorate with felt and sequins. These make nice awards.

31. Make beanbags out of scraps of material. Cut them into various shapes. Some of these can be filled by your group, but some missionaries may prefer that you leave a small opening so that the national can fill it.

32. Make puppets for the missionary to use. Be sure

to make the skin the color of the national in the country to which it is sent. Make a complete family—father, mother, son, daughter, baby, even a grandmother and grandfather. Make garments that can be slipped over the puppet to change it from a modern day father to a Bible character. You can also make paper bag puppets for the missionary to use as awards. These are also good in your own Sunday School. In addition, patterns can be secured from Simplicity (or other pattern companies) for cute animal-shaped puppets. Old stockings can be quickly turned into interesting puppet characters.

33. Do not forget our home missionaries. Many of the items mentioned would be a real help in their work.

20 Prayer Power in Women's Missionary Groups

Prayer is the missionary's most vital need. The world has yet to feel the impact of a women's group that has really caught a glimpse of all that can be wrought by prayer. What would happen in our churches and on mission fields if we *really* believed?

In God's great missionary book, the Acts of the Apostles, we find that the early church and its missionaries asked for God's guidance and power. They followed His leading and were effectively active. They became acquainted with the work, needs and plans of the missionary program of their church. In the church at Antioch, prayer preceded activity. Prayer produced the kind of results that turned many to the Lord. These early Christians were sensitive to the Holy Spirit's leading for their every move.

Our missionary groups will be a glory to the Lord when we, too, become sensitive to the leading of the Holy Spirit. When we begin to wait on the Lord for the selection of our officers, committees and projects, we will see the Lord work in and through our groups. Our nominating committees will not have to search frantically to find talented women with good ideas and organizational abilities. When the women ask with the earnestness of Paul, "Lord, what wilt Thou have me to do?" there will be no shortage of willing workers. When difficulties and problems arise, we will not quit because we will know that God has put us in the difficult place for a purpose.

We must be effectively active in prayer. "Ask, and it

shall be given you . . ." (Matt. 7:7). The promise is ours, but where are the results of our prayers? We open and close meetings with prayer. We ask the blessing on the refreshments and have a missionary prayer time. We believe it is wrong to "say" prayers by using repetitious phrases. We would never consent to ritual. But is it possible that our groups are allowing prayer time to become a mere formality? Do we put our prayers away with the sewing to be brought out at the next meeting? Do we *expect* God to answer, or do we go home to forget what we prayed for at the meeting? Do we pray daily for our missionaries? Do *you* pray daily for your missionaries? Would you dedicate yourself to stand with Samuel who said, "Moreover as for me, God forbid that I should sin against the LORD in ceasing to pray for you . . ." (1 Sam. 12:23)?

What can we do to improve our prayer effectiveness? Be sure to set aside adequate time for prayer. Do not crowd it into the last five minutes. I have attended meetings where the prayer chairwoman read every missionary letter in its entirety. The letters were informative and interesting, but many of the women in the group had received the same letters during the month. The reading took a great deal of time and left little time for the actual prayer portion of the meeting. Prior to the meeting, the prayer chairwoman should read the letters and make a list of all the requests so she can present them during the prayer time.

Prepare prayer cards for each lady to keep in her Bible with a place for requests and a place for answers. Check these cards at each meeting to see if there have been answers to prayer. Add the new requests monthly. Leave space for the member to list personal prayer requests.

You can also make a prayer poster. Put each request on a card and attach it to the prayer poster. When a request is answered, paste a brightly colored seal on the request card and use it in your praise time. Leave the cards on the poster and continue to remember the unanswered requests from month to month. Put the poster on display

105

during each meeting. I am sure there will be great rejoicing at the end of the year when you count up all the answered prayers.

One group has a prayer card file with duplicate cards for each missionary. The card has a picture of the missionary pasted on the corner. Information about the missionary is written on the top of the card, indicating place of service, mission board, family and other helpful information. There is also room for prayer requests to be listed. When a request is answered, it is checked in red. One card remains in the chairwoman's file, and the second card is given to one of the members of the group to use during the prayer time and to take home as her special prayer burden for the coming month. The card is returned at the next meeting and given to another member.

Some groups divide into smaller circles of seven or eight women for the prayer time. A leader is appointed in each group, and she hands the requests to volunteers within the circle. Unless you are well acquainted with all the ladies in the group, be sure to avoid praying around the circle. There are those who are timid about praying in public. Avoid embarrassing anyone present. This type of prayer time has one big advantage—it permits many more women to participate. The chairwoman should make sure that each circle leader is instructed ahead of time and that all the circles know how much time is being allotted for prayer. I once visited a group where this type of circle prayer was used. When the first group finished praying, you could hear them talking and laughing quietly in their corner. By the time the second group was finished, there was a noticeable disturbance. When the third group finished, the women began to move about the room even though the fourth circle was still in prayer. Most of us have personal prayer requests that can be prayed for silently, and the chairwoman should encourage the women to remain in silent prayer until all are finished.

This same incident reminds me of another point. The reason that the fourth group took so long to finish was because one lady prayed methodically across every continent, naming every missionary, bush station, national preacher and political problem. This type of praying is for private devotions. The chairwoman should give this reminder periodically.

Form a missionary prayer chain to care for requests that come during the month. When an emergency arises, a group should begin to pray immediately and not wait for the next monthly meeting.

Do not make a game out of prayer time. There are instances when a group tries to use novel means to increase prayer interest. I once visited a group where the prayer requests had been baked inside a cookie much like the fortune cookie. During the refreshment time the cookie was eaten and the request saved for prayer time. At another meeting, numbered requests were used earlier in the program to award a centerpiece to the lady with request number 12. Our prayer should be guided by the admonition of Ephesians 6:18, "Praying always with all prayer and supplication in the Spirit. . . ." Do not waste your time on trivialities.

You cannot promote prayer any more than you can promote love. Love bubbles forth out of a full heart. You cannot siphon it from an empty heart. Prayer is the cry of faith from a burdened and needy soul. Words are not necessarily prayer even though they are addressed to God.

The officers of a group or the prayer committee chairwoman may organize the prayer time so that everyone is encouraged to pray, even if it is only a sentence prayer. But if this becomes the mere recital of words commonly used in prayer, it is as hypocritical as the careless use of endearing terms. Most of us have had contact with saleswomen who glibly smother us with words of endearment. We allow their chatter to flow into one ear and out the other with little thought because we know they are using idle words. Perhaps God feels somewhat like this when we participate in the prayer session only because we would be embarrassed in front of others

107

if we failed to respond—not because of the burden of our hearts.

Leaders in women's groups should be careful in planning the prayer time. It is quite possible to stretch the time to an hour without much real prayer. I do not want to confuse you. I am in favor of the prayer time in our groups. Nothing is needed more by our missionaries and our churches than earnest prayer. On the other hand, I am concerned that often too much emphasis is put upon what *we* hear rather than what God hears.

Perhaps it would be better if ten or twenty minutes were allowed for prayer. The leader could call upon someone to open the session and ask the chairwoman to close. Those who feel led to do so can pray for requests. If there is a time of silence, do not press the panic button. The chairwoman or leader is not able to tell whether someone is praying silently, but God knows the very thoughts and intents of our hearts. I am sure that there is much soul-searching during these times that seem so awkward to the one in charge. In our desire to have everything click along as planned, we may be hindering the work of the Holy Spirit.

We are prone to judge the outward appearance, but God looks on the heart. I know women who are real prayer warriors, but they are afraid to stand up and pray in a public meeting. Others pray so easily, so long and so thoroughly for every request that anyone who follows them feels that there is nothing left for which to pray. A visitor in the group may be impressed with the woman's knowledge of missions and missionaries, but regular members who hear this recital month after month begin to realize that perhaps it is not so much talking to God as it is an effort to show forth great knowledge. Long prayers should be reserved for private devotions. Public prayers should be to the point, especially if more than one is to pray.

Use God's Word, which is "sharper than any twoedged sword." We have the promise of Jeremiah 33:3, "Call unto me, and I will answer thee, and shew thee great and mighty things, which thou knowest not." If you are a prayer warrior, make your burden a matter of prayer, particularly in private. God will answer and send those to stand with you in prayer.

Testify of answered prayer. Perhaps there are those who think prayer is just a form. Prove to them that it is not a ritual to open and close meetings. Give witness to the miracle-working power of prayer. Often, however, someone will testify as though it was their great faith and faithfulness that brought about answered prayer. Instead, the glory should go to God. He is faithful even when our faith is only the size of a grain of mustard seed.

Stress the importance of private prayer and the need for remembering requests without ceasing during the month. Report the results of answered prayer and give a progress report on requests still unanswered. Once a month public prayer in the women's group is of little consequence if we do not pray and intercede daily for these same requests.

21 The Missionary and the Missionary Group

How can the missionary help the women's missionary group in the local church to be more effective and productive? For the most part, we have always thought of the missionary organization helping the missionary; but until the missionary recognizes his or her part in the successful women's group, there is going to be wasted time and effort for both.

In any great transcontinental business venture, there is always a close tie between home office and foreign representatives. Every department works together to make the effort as effective, productive and profitable as humanly possible. The foreign office keeps the home base informed about market trends and needs so that the highest level of efficiency can be maintained. How much more diligent we should be as we serve the King of kings.

Nearly every missionary has had the disappointment of paying duty on a package or barrel only to find that it is filled with unneeded or unusable items. On the other hand, there are many frustrated officers and committee chairwomen who have been challenged to work for missions but are unable to find projects. If the group is to continue meeting and working, there must be projects, so they roll bandages or turn old shirts into hospital gowns. If they are unaware that some missionaries do not need bandages or hospital gowns, they send them to translators and teachers as well as to dispensary workers and nurses. Both time and postage money are wasted because the missionary

110

has not informed the group of definite needs.

What is the answer? First of all, ask the missionaries to be honest (perhaps a better word is "frank") with you. If the missionary is working among Jewish people in the United States and a women's group sends a large box of pill bottles filled with detergent, the missionary should not write back and say, "Thank you so much for the box of detergent-filled pill bottles. I appreciate all your hard work and interest." I know missionaries do not want to appear ungrateful, but if such packages are accepted without honest comment, groups will continue to send them. When this type of package arrives, the missionary should write to the group and tell them that missionaries in jungle dispensaries or bush stations use soap packed in this fashion; however, your work is with middle-class Jewish people who can afford to buy their own household needs, and you have no need for detergent-filled pill bottles. The missionary can offer to readdress the package to a missionary who needs it if the group sends a name and address and sufficient postage to cover mailing costs. If a project is returned to you, contact the missionary, asking what he *would* like you to do.

When you ask missionaries if they would like certain items made by your group, they should not feel that they have to say yes to prevent hurt feelings. They should explain that they cannot use this type of item on their field or that they already have a sufficient quantity.

Many missionaries are reluctant to give a list of needs to a group for fear that they will appear greedy. This is wrong. Remember, we are laboring together with God. Going is the missionary's duty; supplying his needs is the duty of the women's missionary group. Do not make the missionary feel as if he is begging.

Encourage missionaries to be prepared to answer the question, "What do you need on the mission field that our group can make in work meetings?" because it is sure to be asked in nearly every church. When laywomen hear about the needs on the field, it is only natural that their first question should be, "What can we do to help?" I have asked this question scores of times, and in the majority of cases the missionary has not had an answer except to say, "I will send you a list when I get back home." In most instances the list is not forthcoming, not because the missionary does not have needs but because of lack of time and no preparation for the presentation of needs other than support funds.

Warn your missionaries not to try to handle every individual request for projects with personal letters and lists. Suggest they take a little time and prepare lists before they set out on deputation. It will be time well spent. They should include a list of all the items, both large and small, that are needed on the field. They should also indicate on the list the quantities needed and instructions for making and packing. It is extremely important that detailed mailing or shipping information be given. The list should be presented without apology to a group that asks for it. If the missionary feels that an explanation is necessary, it can be included on the list by simply noting that it covers needs for four years and everything that will be used or worn during that period of time must be taken with the missionary. To avoid an avalanche of any one item, he should suggest that the group notify him when they have selected a project from the list.

Equally important as the list of needs is the list of "I do not need" items. Because most of us think of certain items such as rolled bandages and greeting cards whenever we think of missionaries, it would be well for the missionary to indicate which items cannot be used. If duty or government regulations make it impossible for a missionary to receive packages, that fact should be noted on the information sheet. Saying it while speaking to a church is insufficient because the information may be forgotten.

It is also important for missionaries to remember that it is a poor policy to make fun of articles received from other women's groups. If the knit sweater is knee length and cannot possibly be worn, they should dispose of it, not take it from place to place to show ladies "how not to do it." Some women have been discouraged because of this bit of fun poking, and they no longer work for missionaries. It is better to use a positive approach by showing the group some well-made articles that are a real help and blessing on the field of service.

The third part of the list should be prayer requests. Every missionary has certain basic needs that should be remembered daily, such as spiritual needs, safety, wisdom to deal with nationals, salvation of souls, growth for national Christians, ability to get along with other missionaries, finances, and so on. This list can be left with the officers of a group when the missionary speaks and while the challenge is still fresh in the minds of the ladies. A prayer card should be stapled to the list for easy identification. Some groups will use it primarily as a prayer reminder list and others for both a prayer and project list. If the missionary challenges the group with the need and does not tell them how they can help by supplying needs and praying, he is doing only half the job.

Missions has yet to feel the full impact of what women's groups can do to provide material and prayer support; but unless the missionaries take the time to evaluate their needs and make them known, they will never benefit. Why should they continue to expect "junk" that cannot be used when they can have first-class articles, just for the asking?

The gap that exists between many missionaries and the women's groups in their supporting churches is increasing the cost of sending and keeping missionaries on the field. I know of many, many missionaries who are not asking women's groups to make articles of clothing and other items that are costly when purchased in a store because they are under the impression that women no longer want to sew. On the other hand, there are scores of women's groups who are not sewing because they think that missionaries no longer desire to have them sew.

How was this gap created? I suppose there are many

113

reasons, but I believe one of the greatest causes is a lack of information. Many smaller churches take on only a small portion of a missionary's support, and they see that missionary just a few times during a furlough. After the missionary leaves for the field, the group has its memories and an occasional prayer letter.

It is very important for missionaries to make sure that supporting churches are well informed about their fields, work, families and other personal details. Many missionaries are satisfied if they give supporting churches all the information they request, but they do not want to seem presumptuous; so they hesitate to give information that is not specifically requested. If pastors, missionary committees and women's groups are inexperienced and do not ask for information, the missionary often takes for granted that they do not want it. Many missionaries feel that it is enough to provide information while speaking at a meeting. This is not sufficient, and the information will not be remembered throughout a four-year term of service.

The question is not "How much information does the church want?" It is "How much information can the missionary provide and get the church and its organizations to absorb?" How much information must the church have to make it a dependable source of prayer backing, financial support and material provision? In the interest of the work being done for the Lord on the mission field, the missionary must assume responsibility for informing supporting churches. It is not fair to blame a group for apathy when in reality the problem is created because a missionary has not had an organized, permanent plan for informing supporting churches.

How can the missionary work out an effective program of information? It is not difficult or costly. He should prepare file folders for every supporting church. The missionary should include a supply of prayer cards ready to be mailed upon request. He should write a short but complete biographical sketch of each family member. Then he should prepare information about his field of

114

service, including geographical, climatic, religious, political, educational and cultural aspects. He should also provide information about the mission board, such as location, size, names of director and deputation secretaries, title of mission publication and directions for securing it, doctrinal statement of board, brochures about his field of service that have been published by the mission board and so forth. If he has pictures of his home or church on the mission field or individual pictures of family members, he should include them. Furthermore, he should send family pictures periodically while on the field to keep the churches abreast of growth. This information will help classes, women's groups and members of the church to plan programs that will promote his work while he is on the field. It will also be a means of increasing prayer support. Sunday School departments can use it for missionary Sunday. Program chairwomen can use it for the women's group. The librarian can transfer biographical and other information to notebooks that can be put in the church library for Sunday School children and members to read.

Record sheets are important. The missionary should be sure to include them in the folder so that the church is aware of what can be done for him while he is on the field. He can send additional information and changes in status from time to time and ask that the news be added to the folder that he provided for the church.

Not every missionary will provide information folders; therefore, the local church missionary committee should secure the information from their missionaries at the time they are interviewed by the committee.

The information will not only help the church to do more for its missionaries, but it will also help missionary committees to evaluate individual missionaries who apply for support but who are not serving under mission boards approved by Regular Baptists.

Several of the questions serve as "red flags" if not answered according to the doctrinal stand of the local church. If the missionary has not been commissioned by his local church and is not receiving support from that church, ask him questions before your church assumes a portion of the support. Does the missionary's stand on personal and ecclesiastical separation agree with the stand of your church? Is the missionary under- or oversupported? This information may help you to decide between two missionaries who are serving under the same board but have differing financial needs.

SAMPLE RECORD SHEET

NAME_____BIRTH DATE _____
(month—day—year)
HOME ADDRESS _____PHONE _____

MARITAL STATUS
____Single ____Married ____Widowed ___Divorced
WIFE'S NAME _____BIRTH DATE _____
(month—day—year)
BIRTH DATES
CHILDREN'S NAMES   (month—day—year)
   1._____ _____
   2._____ _____
   3._____ _____
   4._____ _____

EDUCATIONAL INFORMATION (*husband*)
  High School _____Graduation Date ___
  College or University _____Graduation Date ___
  Bible School _____Graduation Date ___
  Seminary _____Graduation Date ___
  Correspondence
   courses completed _____Graduation Date ___
  Other specialized
   training _____Graduation Date ___
  Earned degrees _____
  Ordained _____Where_____Date _____
EDUCATIONAL INFORMATION (*wife*)
  High School _____Graduation Date ___

College or University _____ Graduation Date ____
Bible School _____ Graduation Date ____
Seminary _____ Graduation Date ____
Correspondence
   courses completed _____ Graduation Date ____
Other specialized
   training _____ Graduation Date ____
Earned degrees _____

MISSION BOARD
   Name _____
   Address _____
   Publication _____
PAST SERVICE RECORD
   Names of other boards with which you have served _____

   _____
   Where did you serve? _____

   _____
   How long did you serve under this board? _____
   Reason for terminating service with this board _____

   _____
VETERAN MISSIONARY SERVICE RECORD
   List fields where you have served with present board (*both
   husband and wife*)
   1. _____ Years ____
   2. _____ Years ____
   3. _____ Years ____
   4. _____ Years ____
MISSIONARY APPOINTEE
   Date of appointment by mission board_____
   Length of time on full-time deputation _____
   When do you expect to complete deputation? _____

SUPPORT INFORMATION
   Total personal support
      Needed _____Amount raised _____Date ____
   Total work fund
      Needed _____Amount raised _____Date ____

Total equipment fund
  Needed _____ Amount raised _____ Date ____
Total passage fund
  Needed _____ Amount raised _____ Date ____
Total education fund for children
  Needed _____ Amount raised _____ Date ____
Total rent fund
  Needed _____ Amount raised _____ Date ____
Total other funds
  Needed _____ Amount raised _____ Date ____

DESCRIPTION OF WORK YOU WILL DO ON THE FIELD
(*both husband and wife*)

Teacher _____ Administrator _____
Physician _____ Bible teacher _____
Surgeon_____ Dormitory parents _____
Nurse _____ Literature coordinator _____
Children's worker _____ Musician _____
Construction worker_____ Counselor _____
Translator _____ Housewife _____
Pilot _____ Other _____
Radio operator_____

MISSIONARY SPECIALISTS
If you are specializing, indicate how you plan to carry out the command to "go and preach" (*evangelize*) in addition to your specialty. _____
_____

CHURCH MEMBERSHIP
Name of church and address _____
_____Years ____
                    (*husband*)
Name of church and address _____
_____Years ____
                    (*wife*)
Baptism by immersion
Husband ____Yes ____No   Wife ____ Yes ____No
Testimony of salvation (*include brief statement by both husband and wife*) _____

Testimony of call to missionary service (*include statement by both husband and wife*) _____

Commissioned at _____ Date ____

(Name of church and location)

Description of Christian service prior to acceptance by your mission board

Husband _____

Wife _____

DOCTRINAL

Indicate stand on separation

Personal _____

Ecclesiastical _____

Include doctrinal statement of your home church and mission board (*attach*)

GENERAL INFORMATION

Departure date for field _____ Length of term _____

Expected furlough date _____ Length of term _____

Name and address of friend or relative who can be contacted for information _____

Address of children who are away at school _____

Address of children who are left in United States during term

REPORTING

I plan to send supporting churches (monthly, quarterly or annual) reports indicating the progress of the work on the field; souls reached with the gospel; number of decisions for

The Missionary and the Missionary Group

salvation, baptism, church membership; number of new
churches established; number of Bible classes taught; number of plane flights; descriptions of work being done in other
areas; prayer needs; difficulties; victories.

SUPPORTING CHURCHES
List other supporting churches.
Name   Address

_____
_____
_____
_____
_____
_____
_____
_____
_____
_____

22 The Individual Woman and the Women's Missionary Group

Why are so many ladies' missionary society meetings poorly attended? Churches large and small are concerned because only a small percentage of women are vitally interested in missionary activities. The question most often asked by officers is, "What can we do to create interest?"

Smorgasbords and novel programs will give periodic stimulus to a lagging group, but like any injection treatment, the effect wears off all too soon. Officers can revamp constitutions, improve organization, appoint committees, pep up programs and increase advertising in an effort to promote interest, but it will be to little or no avail unless the women of a church are aware of their responsibility to God for missions. Missionary interest is a personal matter and must be answered by every individual.

In the young people's department, our Sunday School teacher constantly challenged us with this question, "If every member were just like me, what kind of a class would my class be?" Paraphrase that question, "If every woman were just like me, what kind of a missionary group would my church have?" "If every woman were just like me, what kind of material and prayer support would our missionaries have?" The answers to these questions can be found only by prayerful self-examination in the light of God's Word.

Are you helping or hindering your missionary program? Answer the following questions honestly before

121

God, then determine to find your place in His plan to reach every creature with the gospel.

This questionnaire is not intended to be used in a way that women will have to acknowledge failures publicly. Rather it should be filled out privately and failures acknowledged to God (1 John 1:9).

IF EVERY MEMBER WERE JUST LIKE ME, WHAT KIND OF A GROUP WOULD MY GROUP BE?

1. Do you attend regularly?
   Yes _____ No _____
2. Do you arrive on time?
   Yes _____ No _____
3. Do you pray for each meeting before you go?
   Yes _____ No _____
4. Are you willing to be a committee chairwoman or worker on a committee when asked?
   Yes _____ No _____
5. Are you willing to hold an office in your group, trusting God for wisdom and strength?
   Yes _____ No _____
6. Do you know the missionaries supported by your church?
   Yes _____ No _____
7. Do you know where each missionary is working (continent, country, city or village)?
   Yes _____ No _____
8. Do you know about the people among whom your missionary is working (city, jungle, Muslim, Roman Catholic)?
   Yes _____ No _____
9. Do you know what type of work your missionary is doing (medical, evangelistic, teaching, literature, orphanage, Bible class)?
   Yes _____ No _____
10. Do you know your missionaries' work and fields so well that you can think about them day or night and

know they are probably in the operating room doing difficult surgery, in the schoolroom teaching the Word, on a jungle trail going from bush station to bush station, on a launch or plane carrying the gospel, in the city marketplace preaching to those gathered around or perhaps trying to get sleep under a hot mosquito net?
Yes _____ No _____

11. Do you personally correspond with your missionaries?
Yes _____ No _____

12. Do you know and remember the missionaries' personal prayer requests for physical, material and spiritual needs?
Yes _____ No _____

13. Do you *really* believe that every person living on this earth is lost and will pass into an eternal Hell of fire and brimstone without Christ for all eternity unless someone reaches him with the gospel story?
Yes _____ No _____

14. Are you willing to do all you can to equip your missionary in order to make his work as effective as possible so that the greatest number of souls can be reached in the shortest possible time before the end of this age?
Yes _____ No _____

15. Do you believe in prayer?
Yes _____ No _____

16. Would you be shocked if your group dropped its prayer time?
Yes _____ No _____

17. Do you *really* believe John 14:14, "If ye shall ask any thing in my name, I will do it"?
Yes _____ No _____

18. Do you *really* believe the promise of Jeremiah 33:3, "Call unto me, and I will answer thee, and shew thee great and mighty things, which thou knowest not"?
Yes _____ No _____

19. Have you seen great and mighty things happen in answer to your prayers?
Yes _____ No _____

20. Do you remember your missionaries daily in prayer, NOT as a ritual but knowing that God has entrusted to you the responsibility of holding up the arms of His chosen servants?
Yes _____ No _____

21. Do you have a prayer list?
Yes _____ No _____

22. Have you asked God to lay on your heart particular missionaries, particular lost souls and particular needs, and are you praying without ceasing until your prayer is answered whether it takes days, weeks or years?
Yes _____ No _____

23. Can you claim positive answers to your prayers?
Yes _____ No _____

24. Do your missionaries know you are a prayer partner with them?
Yes _____ No _____

25. Do your missionaries have so much confidence in the power of your prayers that they keep you personally informed when they reach a difficult situation or have a specific prayer need?
Yes _____ No _____

26. Do you feel as much called of God to do the work of your missionary group at home as your missionary feels called of God to go to a foreign or home field to serve?
Yes _____ No _____

27. Have you learned to move men by God through prayer?
Yes _____ No _____

28. Do you believe that God will not do for us or our missionaries apart from prayer what He has promised to do through prayer?
Yes _____ No _____

29. Would you ask God to teach you not just *how* to pray

but to teach you *to* pray?
Yes _____No_____

". . . How long are ye slack to go to possess the land, which the LORD God of your fathers hath given you?" (Josh. 18:3).

23 The Pastor's Wife and the Women's Group

Should the pastor's wife hold an office in the women's missionary group? This is a question that cannot be answered with an absolute yes or no. There may be a rare occasion when it is not only wise but also necessary for the pastor's wife to hold an office. Except for these rare occasions, however, I believe that only the laywomen should hold office in the missionary group.

In one mission church that had a congregation of fewer than twenty adults (mostly new Christians), there were only six women in the missionary group, including the pastor's wife. Each of the laywomen was afraid to be president during the organization's first year because of their lack of experience. In this case, it was necessary for the pastor's wife to hold the office in order to get the group started. This is one of the rare occasions when my answer would be, "Yes, it is all right." Under such circumstances, the pastor's wife should advise the ladies that she will serve for one term and that they should be prepared to assume official responsibility at the second election.

One of our churches had the same pastor for nearly thirty-nine years. His wife never held an office, although she was always willing to advise or help the women who were officers or committee chairwomen. She always did her share of the work. In all of those years I never heard one word of criticism about her. On the other hand, I am acquainted with pastors' wives who have been in their churches for just a year or two, and they are in real trouble because they have tried to assume too much authority and leadership responsibility.

I am sure that it must be difficult for the pastor's wife to stand by quietly while we (laywomen) bungle along, making mistake after mistake. One pastor's wife told me that she knew she could do the work easier and more efficiently herself, but she felt it was wiser to wait quietly until she was asked for help. Why? Would it not be better to let the most qualified person assume the authority even if she is the pastor's wife? The following reasons may help to explain why my answer is no.

1. Without a doubt, the majority of pastors' wives may be better qualified than the laywomen. Many of them have had the benefit of Bible school or Bible college training. They have gathered a great deal of knowledge as they have moved from one pastorate to another.

Because the majority of missionary group officers are ordinary ladies who serve for a year or two during their lifetimes, they are afraid to follow an expert in office. There is always the fear that they will not be able to do as good a job as the pastor's wife.

2. At the time of the election, the pastor's wife might have an unfair advantage over a laywoman if her name appeared on the list of nominations. Her special position as the wife of the pastor could cause some women to vote for her on a popularity basis. Some prospective nominees might refuse to run against the pastor's wife. Remember, we are all human.

3. If the group is too dependent on the pastor's wife for leadership, it will fall flat when she leaves to go to another church. We expect our foreign missionaries to set up indigenous churches; thus our home churches need to be indigenous too.

The pastor's wife should be ready to act in an advisory capacity to all the women in the group but especially to the officers and committee chairwomen. Some pastors' wives keep a file of suggestions, articles, projects and patterns to be used to help when necessary. Many women fearful of holding an office will appreciate knowing they can turn to the pastor's wife for assistance.

All this reminds me of a little bit of poetry that I wrote several years ago.

IF she can be humble without flaunting her humility;

IF she can be a leader without being boss;

IF she can be talked to without being a talker;

IF she can be righteous without being self-righteous;

IF she can create Vogue fashions from inexpensive remnants;

IF she can be a silent observer when she is dying to tell them how;

IF she can move into a scrumptious parsonage without deciding to remain forever;

IF she can turn a rickety church house into a home;

IF she can listen to the preacher's sermons without being proud;

IF she can stand having her P.K.'s watched and criticized for being human;

IF she can admire the parishioners' new appliances and cars without a twinge of e`nvy;

IF she can be grateful for the wallpaper covered with giant roses in the tiny dining room;

IF she can attend every meeting, help the preacher call, counsel the troubled and still keep her house spotlessly clean;

IF she can serve gourmet meals on a hamburger budget;

IF she can be prepared constantly for unexpected guests;

IF she can be sweet and friendly to the ornery deacon who gives her husband hives at the board meeting;

IF she can sing, teach, speak, play or pray when asked and only then;

SHE is the preacher's wife!

It is quite evident that there can be a lack of communication between the women of a church and the pastor's wife. In some instances it is plain that the pastor's wife in a new church situation is timid about making suggestions, and the women of the church are afraid to put too much pressure on her. Unwittingly, a communication gap is created.

On the other hand, a pastor's wife may on occasion come before the ladies, filled with ideas from a previous pastorate. She expects to remodel the group and causes dissension between herself and the group's officers. Likewise, many groups are at fault because they do not want a new person—even the pastor's wife—telling them what to do. This attitude creates a breach that may never heal.

Can these situations be avoided? Certainly! We are serving the Lord. Our purpose is to provide the best possible prayer and material support for our missionaries. It does not make a great deal of difference, therefore, whether the ideas are ours or those of someone else. It is easy for some women to become a little edgy (or more to the point, it is easy for some to develop petty jealousies). We humans do not like to see someone else trample our ideas or past efforts underfoot, and a few ladies wear their feelings on their sleeves. Such tendencies should be avoided, for Satan can use them to good advantage.

Can you imagine a large, progressive company bringing an aggressive, capable, well-trained man into its organization and then informing him that he is not to refer to his past experience or try in any way to change the operation? Of course not! A thriving business takes every opportunity available to gather new ideas and suggestions to make increased efficiency and growth possible.

When the wife of the new pastor comes to your church or new members unite with your group, plan an idea exchange meeting. The president should moderate the meeting and explain the group's organization and purpose. She can also introduce the new members and invite them to join in every part of the women's work. In the case

129

of the new pastor's wife, the group may want to present a corsage to her and give her an official welcome. It may be helpful if all the women wear name tags for this special occasion. Do not take for granted that the pastor's wife knows she is invited to attend the meeting. I know of one instance where the group was offended because the pastor's wife did not come to the meetings. On the other hand, the pastor's wife was offended because she had never been invited to attend.

At such a meeting you can have the pastor's wife or the new women join the officers on a panel to discuss the different phases of a women's missionary group. The new members could explain how their former groups handled each area. Women in the group can add their suggestions. Some women will respond without prodding, but others will need to be asked definite questions; for instance, "What type of program did you have in your group?" "Did you have a program committee?" "Did your group use printed program material?" "What method did you use to determine the needs of the missionaries?"

Appoint a secretary to record the ideas and suggestions. The officers can then meet to discuss them and decide which ones would be beneficial to the group. File other ideas for future reference and use. Do not enter into debate to prove why the ideas will not work in your group. It would be a good idea for women's groups to conduct this type of meeting periodically, even if there are no new members.

Invite your pastor's wife to attend the officers' meetings when she has time. Give her an opportunity to express her opinions. She will appreciate this courtesy. If she works with you in this way, she will be in a better position to advise officers who need help. And she can help them without running the risk of interfering. It is best for the pastor's wife to serve all officers in an advisory capacity rather than to hold one office. If you do not offer her an opportunity to voice her opinions in the planning meetings, it may appear to others that she is interfering when she speaks up at the business meeting of the group.

Join hands with your pastor's wife in an effort to serve the Lord in the best possible way instead of jockeying for the top position or the last word. Welcome new people, ideas and methods; and you will add new energy, enthusiasm and accomplishment to your group.

You may need to prime the pump just a bit at your first idea exchange meeting. Use some of the questions in "A Checklist for Your Women's Group." Officers should be very careful that they do not become defensive during the discussion. For instance, if you are discussing question number seven about short business meetings and someone suggests that your business meetings are too long, do not show offense or respond curtly. Rather begin a discussion on ways to shorten the meetings. Find out what the concensus is among the ladies. It is possible for officers not to realize that the business sessions have been getting longer. If someone suggests that you could just as well dispense with reports, take the opportunity to explain the importance of such reports. Let the women know that you are not making decisions on these questions at that meeting, so there will be no voting. Rather the officers will meet to discuss all the suggestions and those that are workable will be incorporated into future meetings.

Many women's groups are asking, "Why is there such a lack of interest in our meetings?" "What is wrong with our group?" "When did we get into a rut?" "Where can we find answers to our problems?" "Who is responsible?"

Answering these questions is not the purpose of the checklist. All too often we take aspirin tablets to relieve recurring headaches when what we really need most is a thorough physical examination to discover the underlying cause of pain. If your group is at odds with your pastor's wife or other new members in the group, be sure to check thoroughly for the cause. You may find the answer to many other problems.

24 The Women's Group and Missionary Education in the Church

The women's group can do a great deal to help with the promotion of missionary education in the church and Sunday School. The women's group is an arm of the church, and before projects of this type are started, the officers should clear them with the pastor, missionary committee and Sunday School superintendent. Many problems can arise if a group oversteps its bounds and gets into another organization's sphere of responsibility. The women's group can supply the Sunday School with materials to use to increase interest in missions. They will probably welcome your help and interest. The following suggestions may be of help.

1. SCRAPBOOKS—Make colorful scrapbooks to give to Sunday School students so that they can prepare missionary notebooks. Stories and pictures that relate to the church's missionaries can be clipped from newspapers and magazines. For example: "Monsoon Rains Hit Bangladesh"; "Earthquake Shocks Guatemala"; "War Erupts in Cambodia"; "United States Relations with China Improved." Below the article or picture the student can indicate how the event affects missions in that area. A monsoon in Bangladesh could prompt the following concerns for prayer and action:
   a. Safety of national churches.

b. Plight of Christians whose homes have been destroyed.
c. Condition of mission property.
d. Disease caused by flooding and lack of sanitation.
e. Is there a need for emergency medical supplies?
f. Will the nationals lose earning power because places of employment have been destroyed?
g. Will the government care for its people, or will the missionary be involved in restoration and rehabilitation?
h. Have transportation and communication been interrupted?
i. Will the missionary need additional funds?

This project will help the membership consider the role of current events and world trends on the life and work of missionaries. It can also instill an awareness of the responsibility of the church to the missionary.

2. POSTER CONTEST—Interdepartmental contests can be conducted in several categories:
a. Need for missions (Scriptural commission)
b. Information about particular fields
c. Information about branches of mission work (medical, teaching, etc.)
d. Role of the church in missions
e. Role of the layperson in missions

Judge the posters on content, aptness, neatness, originality, etc. Names and other identifying marks should be on the back of the posters so the judging can be unbiased. Display the posters in each department of the Sunday School and on the church bulletin boards. Prizes that have been made by the women's group may be awarded. These need not be large or expensive.

3. MISSIONARY BOARD—If you do not have a board, make an attractive display of missionary pictures

and a world map. Be sure to keep the pictures up-to-date.

4. TAPES—Send each missionary a blank tape with the request that it be returned with a greeting to the church. If your tape recorder is reel to reel or has adjustable speed, indicate the speed that your tape recorder plays so that the missionaries' tapes can be made accordingly. The church can also send tapes of meetings and sermons as well as personal greetings to the missionaries. This project will help the membership to become better acquainted with the missionaries and their work.

5. CURIO DISPLAYS—Start a display cabinet in your church. Appoint a different committee to be in charge of the display each month and assign a different missionary for each month. Allow each committee several months to plan a display. It takes time to think of a meaningful theme as well as to secure curios and articles that will create interest. You can ask young people of the church to work with you on the displays. This is excellent training for them.

6. MISSIONARY NEWS—Have a committee review all of the letters from the missionaries, condense them and mimeograph them in a monthly paper. Include the missionaries' names, fields of service, boards and the names of family members. If they have relatives in the church, list them so that the congregation can associate the missionary with the church family. Each month one missionary could be featured in a biographical sketch. Include birthdays and addresses so cards can be sent. Distribute these papers to all members of the church and Sunday School.

25 The Women's Group and the Church Missionary Conference

In many churches the missionary conference is an annual event, and the women's group usually becomes quite involved with the planning, preparation and displays. As soon as committees are appointed, the members begin to ask questions and to search for new ideas.

The missionary conference involves much work, but it can also be a great deal of fun. The selection of the steering committee is vital. Appoint those who are interested in missions and who have the ability to think creatively and to organize. They should be faithful in completing tasks and willing to expend effort to see results. Congregations are often blamed for apathy and lack of interest when in reality the problem is poor planning. Many churches do not prepare the congregation for the missionary conference. Apart from publicizing the names of speakers and the conference dates, very little is done. In addition, many committees are reluctant to put forth more than the "least effort." They take care of a few routine duties and feel that their responsibility has been discharged. Others excuse their lack of effort by dogmatically claiming that anyone who is interested in missions will attend without all the extra frills. These attitudes and practices invariably result in poorly attended meetings. The women in the missionary group can do much to overcome these problems if they are enthusiastic and if they are willing to assume responsibility for some of the extra features.

135

The following ideas are a few of many that can be used to make a conference draw even the hard-to-get crowd. Implementing these suggestions will be worthwhile.

1. Use preconference projects to stimulate interest. (Some of the projects listed in the chapter on "The Women's Group and Missionary Education in the Church" can be used during the weeks prior to the conference.)

2. Secure speakers well in advance of the conference. Confer with them about your plans and ask for ideas.

3. Plan preconference prayer meetings. These are just as important as when preparing for special evangelistic meetings.

4. Use music to develop interest and prepare hearts. Ask the song leader to use at least one missionary number each Sunday for several weeks prior to the conference; have the choir prepare special missionary numbers (possibly a missionary cantata); introduce missionary songs and choruses in the Sunday School.

5. Conduct a poster contest.

6. Promote an essay contest. High school, college and adult departments can compete on an assigned subject relating to missions. (One missionary was called to the mission field through such writing.)

7. Encourage children and adults to read books about missions. Publish a list of books available in the church library; display book jackets of missionary books on the bulletin board; encourage members or groups to donate new missionary books to the library.

8. Involve people. Those who participate in preparation, almost without exception, are faithful in attendance. It is better to have five ten-member committees than it is to have one twenty-member

committee.

9. Appoint a publicity committee. The best possible program can be planned, but unless it is advertised, the attendance will be small. Begin the publicity well in advance of the conference. Start at the local church level and branch out to the community so that everyone has the opportunity to hear or see at least one attention-getting announcement. We often think of the missionary conference as being for Christians only. However, it can also be a means of reaching the unsaved.

10. Appoint a nursery committee. Prepare for the care of toddlers and infants at every meeting.

11. Appoint a telephone and transportation committee. Enlist a corps of women from your missionary group to call members and friends of the church and Sunday School. (Call everybody even though they attend regularly and see the announcements every week. It is the personal contact that counts.) Remind them of the approaching conference and special events. Offer transportation if it is needed.

12. Appoint a display committee. It should meet as soon as it is appointed to decide the type of displays to be used. Vary them from year to year. The following suggestions may be helpful.

    a. Booths—You can plan one or two or even fifty booths, depending upon the space available and the vim, vigor and vision of the committee. The booths can be tabletop-size or as large as eight feet by eight feet if materials are available. The frame should be made of wood, but the sides can be made from large refrigerator-size cardboard boxes.

    b. Auditorium displays—Consider platform displays instead of booths. Several committees would be responsible for different displays. Each evening the display can be changed to depict the country or continent represented by the speaker. Although this type of decoration is up for only one night, it is very impressive.

c. Table displays—These can be interesting if well planned. Do not settle for a few pieces of literature and some curios.

d. Include displays for all the missionaries supported by your church as well as displays for the countries represented by the speakers at the conference.

e. Include displays for the Sunday School and other departments of the church that are missionary in their outreach to the community.

f. Distribute souvenirs at each booth: a stamp from a foreign country; Jewish cookies at the Jewish mission booth; a coffee bean from Brazil.

g. The displays should be informative as well as decorative. Research economic and religious conditions in the countries represented.

h. Use slides of a missionary's work at the display booth or table.

i. Use recorded greetings from the missionary who is still on the field.

j. Whenever possible, have members of the missionary's family present in the booth to meet visitors.

k. Secure tapes or records of music to use at the booths. (For instance, play Japanese music at the Japanese booth. Many libraries carry records of the Jewish Passover celebration, and one can be played at the Jewish mission booth.)

13. Appoint a special events committee.

a. Family night carry-in supper. Use disposable table service so everyone can attend the meeting.

b. Dessert smorgasbord. Have ladies bring favorite desserts after the Friday evening meeting. Guide the missionary from group to group.

c. Tea or luncheon for ladies and daughters. Use a woman missionary as the speaker.
d. Breakfast for men and boys. This is a good Saturday morning event when the missionary can speak in a less formal way.
e. Youth pizza party after church on Sunday evening. The young people can become acquainted with the missionary as a person.
f. Round-table discussions or seminars can be held during the day to discuss assigned subjects. This could be a time when the women of the missionary group spends time with the missionaries.

14. Children, young people and some adults will enjoy wearing costumes.
15. Teach the children a chorus in a foreign language.

All of these ideas cannot be used at one conference. Choose, therefore, the suggestions that can be employed at your church. Whatever you do, do it well.

26 Women's Meeting in the Wilderness (Skit)

INSTRUCTIONS: This program can be read by one person, but it is most effective when the parts for the different characters are assigned to ladies in the group.

    The skit can be presented with the characters seated among the women and the president at the podium as in a regular meeting. Or chairs may be arranged at the front of the room for each of those participating. Have a small table at which the president and secretary are seated.

    The program can be made more interesting if the characters are dressed to represent the women of Moses' time. Long strips of material can be wrapped around the women to cover their heads and bodies in the fashion of a sari.

NARRATOR (*standing at one side of stage area*): I would like to have you visit a women's group with me. We are going to leave this meeting and the twentieth century and slip back through the years—yes, back through the centuries to the time of Moses. It is very hot and dusty here. We are in the wilderness. The meeting is in that tent over there. We are a little late . . . they have started already. The secretary is reading the minutes. Listen!

SECRETARY: ". . . And the meeting was adjourned. Respectfully submitted, Naomi." (*Secretary pauses briefly, closes notebook and looks at group.*) I want to thank my sister, Naomi, for helping me last month. She read the minutes for me and took the notes so I could attend my pottery class. If it hadn't been for her, I would have missed out on the class, and it cost me eighty shekels. I don't mind missing if something else is more important, but, well, I am sure you all understand. Thanks, Naomi.

PRESIDENT: Thank you. Are there any additions or corrections? If not, the minutes stand approved as read. May we have the treasurer's report?

TREASURER: I forgot to bring it along, and I can't even remember how much we have in the treasury. We will just have to wait until next month for a report or to disburse any funds.

PRESIDENT: May we have the report of the nominating committee?

CHAIRWOMAN: We are having a very difficult time trying to get anyone to hold an office. Nearly everyone is willing to back the new officers, but they are unwilling to accept the responsibility of leadership. I wonder if there is anyone here who would volunteer to hold one of the offices *(pauses for twenty or thirty seconds)*? Well, I don't know what we will do, but perhaps we can meet again as a committee. If you have any ideas, let me know.

PRESIDENT: I received this letter from Moses. I am sure he is no stranger to any of us here in this meeting. I am not going to read all of it to you because it is quite lengthy, but this is the important part: "The Lord has said, 'Bring me an offering: of every man that giveth it willingly with his heart ye shall take my offering. And this is the offering which ye shall take of them; gold, and silver, and brass, and blue, and purple, and scarlet, and fine linen, and goats' hair, and rams' skins dyed red, and badgers' skins, and shittim wood, oil for the light, spices for anointing oil, and for sweet incense, onyx stones, and stones to be set in the ephod, and in the breastplate. And let them make

me a sanctuary; that I may dwell among them' "
(Exod. 25:1–8). He signed it "Moses." (*Heaves a
sigh.*)

I know this is a big order, but I think we ought to
be as obedient as possible in carrying out the plans
for building the tabernacle. I have talked it over with
some of the wives of the leaders, and they all feel that
it would be impossible to expect the people to give all
the things listed in this communication from Moses.
(*Fold letter and lay it on the table. Leah, who is sitting
on front row, will step up and take it back to her seat
where she continues to read it to herself.*) I do feel that
we should do *something*. If we don't do our best, it will
certainly make it appear that we are not concerned
or interested, and this will give our group a bad
image. Rebekah, did you have something to say?

REBEKAH: I am sure that there must be a reason for this
to be brought up at this time—I mean about bringing
all these gifts. I have been taking an arts and crafts
course, and I am conscious of all that can be done
with things that we would otherwise throw away. I
have noticed some perfectly good things going to
waste, and you know me, I just can't bear to see
anything wasted. It won't be long and I am going to
have to buy a tent just to keep things in (*pauses and
chuckles*).

I would like to suggest that we collect as many old
manna buckets as we can spare. They can be turned
into beautiful trivia. Also, you know the bits of straw
that were left over from brick-making? Well, I am
sure we can find a use for these if we just put our
heads together and think. Then there are those who
have old bullock horns lying around. Why not bring
those if you have no other use for them? Oh, yes, we
may not need this, but I would suggest that you bring
any old scraps of cloth or old clothing just in case we
can't afford all those fine linen curtains. I think that we
could make some attractive patchwork curtains that

would do just as well. Thank you, madam president.
That's all I have to say; just a few ideas.

SECRETARY *(speaks from seat)*: I, for one, do appreciate
Rebekah and her wonderful ideas.

PRESIDENT: I am pleased with your ideas, too, Rebekah.
I am sure that you are aware that we all look to you
for those clever suggestions that you always seem to
know about. If any of you have any gifts that you can
spare or any time that you can give out of your busy
lives to work on the project, please see our project
chairwoman about Moses' request so the committee
can be thinking about it and making plans. Would
the project chairwoman please give her report at this
time?

PROJECT CHAIRWOMAN: There is a need for ten curtains
of fine-twined linen, blue and purple and scarlet with
cherubims of cunning work.

MIRIAM *(jumps to her feet and interrupts)*: Has a committee been appointed to investigate cheaper curtains?
*(Remains standing while project chairwoman an-
swers.)*

PROJECT CHAIRWOMAN *(hesitates and fumbles for first
word)*: Well, I am just a little surprised by your
question, Miriam. We have not investigated cheaper
curtains because we felt that the instructions Moses
gave were so clear and definite.

MIRIAM *(speaks with authority)*: I move that a committee
be appointed to call all of the women to see if they
have leftover materials, and if that fails, the committee should be instructed to go down to the Wilderness
Bargain Basement to see what is on sale.

ORPAH: I second the motion. I don't see why the material
has to be so fine twined. Another thing—I don't think
it is very wise to waste our time and money on
cunning work and cherubims.

DEBORAH: Do you know why they are insisting on blue,
purple and scarlet for the curtains? Pink, orange and
yellow material will no doubt be on sale because they

143

were last year's colors. I really don't think color should make too much difference because those curtains are just going to get dirty and dusty out there in the desert. (*Sits slowly when Ruth interrupts.*)

RUTH: Those who are doing the planning of the tabernacle have surely lost sight of the fact that they are spending God's money. I am a very conscientious person, you all know that I am, surely, and it grieves me (*dabs eye with handkerchief*) when we carelessly waste our money on finery and extravagance. My husband Simon and I always say, "We spend God's money just the way we do our own." (*Appears pious, cocks head and sits down.*)

PRESIDENT (*pounds table with gavel*): Ladies, ladies, we have a motion on the floor and a second. Are you ready to vote? Perhaps we should hear the motion again. Will the secretary read it?

SECRETARY: Miriam moved that a committee be appointed to call all of the women to see if they have leftover materials, and if that fails, the committee should be instructed to go down to the Wilderness Bargain Basement to see what is on sale. Seconded by Orpah.

PRESIDENT: All those in favor, please raise your right hand. All those opposed, same sign. (*Looks the audience over as if counting.*) The motion has carried unanimously. As soon as I can find time, I will appoint a committee to investigate a cheaper way to make the curtains. Now, I will turn the meeting back to the project chairwoman. (*She is still standing with her paper in her hand.*)

PROJECT CHAIRWOMAN (*with offended air*): We already *have* material enough for ten curtains, and we need ten women to take them home for hemming. The instructions say: "The length of one curtain shall be eight and twenty cubits, and the breadth of one curtain four cubits: and every one of the curtains shall have one measure" (Exod. 26:2). My own personal feelings are that the tabernacle committee will have to take what they can get. Just make them as close as possible to these measurements, but don't worry about a few inches more or less, one way or the other. These curtains will no doubt be flapping out there in the wind anyway, and no one will notice a short curtain or two.

PRESIDENT: Is that all from the project chairwoman? Now the handwork committee has a report for us.

HANDWORK COMMITTEE CHAIRWOMAN: I will begin by saying that all of the members of my committee are upset about the instructions for loops. Just listen: "Make loops of blue upon the edge of the one curtain from the selvedge in the coupling; and likewise shalt thou make in the uttermost edge of another curtain, in the coupling of the second. Fifty loops shalt thou make in the one curtain, and fifty loops shalt thou make in the edge of the curtain that is in the coupling of the second; that the loops may take hold one of another" (Exod. 26:4, 5) (*sighs and shakes head*). I am really quite indignant. I feel the tabernacle committee is taking unfair advantage of our women. I have been doing some figuring on papyrus, and as far as I can see, we don't need anywhere near that many loops. If the men on the committee were doing the work themselves, they wouldn't demand so many. If we put the loops farther apart, like this (*measures distance with hands*), we can get along with half of what they say is needed. I am not trying to be fussy, but all those loops and clasps are monkey business and a waste of time. Besides that (*starts wiping brow with handkerchief and voice begins to quiver*), the doctor has just put me on tranquilizers and suggested that I cut down on my activities (*sits down*).

LEAH (*Leah, who is still reading Moses' letter, suddenly gasps and hits the side of her head with her hand*): You haven't heard anything yet; just listen to this: "And for the gate of the court shall be an hanging of

145

twenty cubits, of blue, and purple, and scarlet, and fine twined linen, *wrought with needlework*" (Exod. 27:16). Now I don't want to appear cri ical, but I don't even have fancy needlework in *my own home.* Why should I do it for the Tabernacle? I think this is an imposition and a waste of time; besides my husband does not like the idea of my being gone from the tent so much. He feels that the older women should do this kind of thing because they don't have young children to take care of all day.

REBEKAH: My husband feels the direct opposite. He says the younger women should take their turn and let some of the older women rest. We have been doing the work for years. Someone else should take a turn. Besides that, Joseph has retired and we are going to get out of this arid place for a few months.

PRESIDENT (*pounds gavel*): Ladies, is there any more old business?

CHAIRWOMAN OF COURT SURVEY COMMITTEE: Madam president, you appointed us to serve on a committee to survey the proposed size of the court of the tabernacle. I would like to report on what we have done up to now. We talked to Moses, and he said that the length should be one hundred cubits, the breadth fifty cubits and the height five cubits, *and all of fine twined linen.* Our committee feels that this is just too big. They will never use it. It will be wasted space. If all of the men on that committee are like my husband, they probably didn't do much thinking while they were doing the planning. My husband built a doghouse last year, and it was so big that the whole family, including my mother-in-law, could have lived in it comfortably.

MEMBER OF COURT SURVEY COMMITTEE: You had better remind them again that it calls for *fine twined linen.* It's busy work; that's all it is (*mumbles last sentence, but clearly enough to be heard*).

MEMBER OF GOATS' HAIR CURTAIN COMMITTEE: I am

146

not the chairwoman of the goats' hair curtain committee, but I have been asked to give you a report on what we have been doing. Our chairwoman was unable to be present because her Uncle Aaron came to spend a few days, and she couldn't very well leave him alone. We are supposed to make eleven goats' hair curtains, measuring thirty cubits long and four cubits wide each. We haven't made much progress. In fact, we really haven't done anything. We have not been able to get the committee together to pick out the material. One of the members has been busy preparing for the Garden Club Tour to Babylon, and she hasn't had a minute and won't have until she returns and recovers. They purchased a Camel-Air-Van-Travel-All, you know. If they are going to get their money's worth, they feel they should use it at every opportunity. (*She pauses.*) If we had one, I probably would go too. (*She laughs.*)

Another member of our committee had an opportunity to go with her husband on a business trip to Canaan. She just couldn't turn it down. She told me that she felt it must be God's will that she do some shopping and personal things.

The third member of our committee has small children, and they have had so many music lessons, sports events and doctor appointments that she hasn't had a minute. Our chairwoman doesn't feel we can condemn her for being interested in her children. After all, the future of the tabernacle will rest upon the shoulders of these little ones. If they learn to hate the tabernacle because their mother is too active and they are deprived of her attention an hour or two a month, it could have lasting effects.

Let's see, there is another member on the committee—oh, my goodness, it's me. Well, girls, you know I am quite humble and not one for going ahead on my own. I'm not too talented, you know. If someone tells me what to do, I try. I guess we don't have

147

Women's Meeting in the Wilderness (Skit)

too much to report now. Besides, we all think it is too big a project anyway.

PRESIDENT (*glances into corner*): Ladies, I see by the sundial that our time has slipped by and we are not going to be able to pursue our reports any further or have a work meeting. Perhaps all the talk about projects that need to be done is a little premature because we are not going to be able to have a work meeting for at least ten months. I am going to let our program committee chairwoman tell you what they have planned.

PROGRAM CHAIRWOMAN (*very enthusiastically*): At each of our meetings for the next ten months we are going to have special speakers. They are going to tell us about their experiences during the ten plagues and how it affected them and their families psychologically. They will bring curios and show slides of the events. Refreshments will be served at each of the meetings, of course (*everyone claps*).

PRESIDENT: Doesn't that sound delightful? I knew you would be enthusiastic. You know what they say about "Women in the Wilderness." They can't meet without eating. Try to bring your friends and neighbors. Today our refreshment committee has planned a delicious smorgasbord. We do appreciate the hours and hours of time that the committee puts into serving tasty refreshments at each of our meetings. I am sure that we go home quite distended from overeating. Now, let me see, have we taken care of everything? Yes, I believe we have. Did you have something to say, Orpah?

ORPAH: What about the offering?

PRESIDENT: Do you remember that we voted last month to eliminate this month's offering because most of us are a little short after all the gift buying during the holidays? But don't forget we will have an offering next month.

LEAH: I move we adjourn.

148

PRESIDENT: All those in favor stand, and we will proceed to the smorgasbord table.

NARRATOR: As we have watched this skit, most of us have laughed. These events did not happen in the wilderness, but the failures they represent can occur today in all of our women's groups. Why? Were the women of that day different? No, they just feared God. They knew about the judgments that fell upon those who dared to disobey His command. They had gone to the mount with Moses to meet God. They saw the great God of the universe descend in fire and smoke. They felt the mountain quake because of the presence of God. They knew that God always judges sin and disobedience. Memories of the plagues were written upon the hearts of even the very young as the stories of God's dealing with Pharaoh were told over and over again.

Has God changed? Is He less righteous, less holy, less interested in the obedience of His people? Does He expect Christians to obey His commands? Can we ignore the instructions He gives us just because we are saved by grace? Do you think God looks lightly on us when we ignore His commission to "Go ye into all the world, and preach the gospel to every creature"? Do we treat His command to us lightly because we do not KNOW God?

We need women and Christians whose hearts have been stirred and whose spirits have been made willing. (Read Exodus 35:21–29; 36:1–3.)

When we, too, come with stirred spirits and willing hearts, there will be no lack among our missionaries. Appointees will not be waiting several years to secure support. There will be no closed dispensaries, unconstructed churches and work not done on our mission stations because we have failed at home. Instead our mission boards will send word to us to hold up on the giving—the people have brought more than enough to carry on the work, just as they did when the tabernacle was being built (Exod. 36:4–7).

Our need today is for stirred spirits and willing hearts. These can be ours—just for the asking. God has promised: "Call unto me, and I will answer thee, and shew thee great and mighty things, which thou knowest not."

27 A Checklist for Your Women's Group

	Yes	No
1. Do you start on time?	____	____
2. Do your officers and committees arrive on time?	____	____
3. Are the work and equipment laid out before the meeting?	____	____
4. Do you greet and make welcome those who come to the meetings, especially the newcomers?	____	____
5. Do you invite women through personal contact, posters, announcements, bulletin inserts, telephone calls, letters?	____	____
6. Do you contact those who were absent at previous meetings to let them know they were missed?	____	____
7. Are your business meetings short, interesting and to the point?	____	____
8. Do members feel free to participate in the business meetings?	____	____
9. Do your work committees have their projects well planned?	____	____
10. Is there variety in work projects so that women who cannot sew or quilt can cut cards, roll bandages, etc.?		
11. Do you work on known needs of the missionary instead of hoping the		

Yes   No

missionary will need what you are
working on?

12. Do your work committees keep a
record of work taken home by members?

13. Are you aware of home as well as
foreign missions, including needs
for the summer Bible school, Sunday School, etc.?

14. Are you careful about sending only
good used clothing and articles?

15. Are the offerings in your group sufficient to purchase quality materials?

16. Is work given or sent to the missionary as soon as it is done?

17. Do you keep a record of work done
by your group so that you can report
to the group the accomplishments
of the year?

18. Do you consider the cost of postage
before you start a project? (Many
groups make boxes and boxes of
rolled bandages but cannot afford to
send them.)

19. Do you follow packing and mailing
instructions for the country to which
you are mailing?

20. Do you have variety in your programming?

21. Do you pay your missionary
speaker's travel expenses and baby-
sitter's fees when they are incurred?

22. Do you have missionary speakers
when they are available—not as en-
tertainers, but as informers so you
will be better able to pray and work?

23. Is there any effort on the part of your

Chapter 27

Yes   No

group to interest young women, girls
and children in missions? ____ ____

24. Do you have a program for acquaint-
ing the women in your group with
facts and figures about missionary
fields and the work being done by
our mission boards around the world? ____ ____

25. Do you know the inroads being made
by cults, isms and the political up-
heavals on the mission fields? ____ ____

26. Does your group and its officers
have a real vision of missions and
the part they have been called to fill
in order to carry out the Great
Commission? ____ ____

27. Do you make available to your group
literature and missionary news from
your missionaries and their boards? ____ ____

28. Are the women of your group willing
to hold office and accept committee
appointments? (Pastors' wives are
often forced into offices when they
would prefer acting in an advisory
capacity.) ____ ____

29. Do your officers meet to plan prayerfully the activities of your group? ____ ____

30. Do you have a purpose for having a
missionary group? (Some groups
are missionary in name and ladies'
aid in function.) ____ ____

31. Do you have a constitution? ____ ____

32. Does your group correspond with
the missionaries? ____ ____

33. Do you have an adequate prayer
time? ____ ____

34. Do you have a missionary prayer
card system so that requests can be

Yes No

remembered by the ladies during
the month? ___ ___

35. Do you have an emergency prayer
chain for requests that come to you
between meetings? ___ ___

36. Do you acknowledge prayer answers? ___ ___

37. Do you remember to pray for your
officers and activities? ___ ___

38. Are your officers and committees
faithful to their tasks? (Many times
absentee habits of those in charge
cause members to be careless too.) ___ ___

39. Are your officers and committees
enthusiastic in the way they carry
out their duties? ___ ___

40. Are you willing to seek the Lord's
guidance as you seek to overcome
the weaknesses of your group? ___ ___